THE SUNBONNET FAMILY OF QUILT PATTERNS

1a

2a

3a

4a

THE SUNBONNET FAMILY OF QUILT PATTERNS

DOLORES A. HINSON

ARCO PUBLISHING, INC.
NEW YORK

Other books by Dolores A. Hinson

QUILTING MANUAL
A QUILTER'S COMPANION
A SECOND QUILTER'S COMPANION
AMERICAN GRAPHIC QUILT DESIGNS
QUILTS FOR BABIES AND CHILDREN

Published by Arco Publishing, Inc.
215 Park Avenue South, New York, N.Y. 10003

Library of Congress Cataloging in Publication Data

Hinson, Dolores A.
    The sunbonnet family of quilt patterns.

    Includes index.
    1. Quilting—Patterns. I. Title.
TT835.H53 1983   746.46′041′0973   83-7113
    ISBN 0-668-05864-1 (Cloth Edition)
    ISBN 0-668-05987-7 (Paper Edition)

Printed in the United States of America

10   9   8   7   6   5   4   3   2   1

Front jacket: "Dutch Dolls Quilt," made by Louise Spence for her daughter Betty Stroud in the 1930's. Collection of Betty Stroud. Photograph by Jim Nash.

Back jacket: Lindsay Noel Friedman photographed in "Mary Christmas" jumper; photograph by Susan Sammis. "Sunbonnet Baby Quilt," pink wall hanging, unquilted blue wall hanging made by and in the collection of Beverly A. Orbelo; pink Sunbonnet pillow in the collection of Mr. and Mrs. Hull Youngblood; Snow Child hoop hanging, designed by Dolores A. Hinson, made by and in the collection of Diane Herbort; photography by Jim Nash.

Contents

Foreword

While sorting out my quilt patterns and grouping them by subject, I found a great number of Sunbonnet types, which caught my attention and finally prompted the writing of this pattern book. In recent years a wide range of Sunbonnet designs—including the Overall Boy patterns as well—have been neglected in favor of one basic form that has been used to the exclusion of all variations. This does tend to promote boredom. The many diverse patterns given in this volume are intended to bring others of the type back into favor. For children and for certain decorating situations, the small people gathered in these patterns make very pleasing designs.

Sunbonnet designs defy rigid classification. When these patterns have been named at all, they have usually been called simply Sunbonnet Sue or Overall Bill. On the other hand, after the fad of the 'twenties for Dutch designs, *all* Sunbonnet patterns began to be referred to as "Dutch Dolls" across the American South. I have grouped younger figures, especially those of fairly plain design, those shown wearing work or play clothes, and those for which the clothes are not a primary focus of interest as Sunbonnet Babies, after the earliest Bertha Corbett figures (see page 7). Patterns featuring fancy-dress or period costumes I have called Colonial Ladies (there is one Colonial Gentleman), especially when the figures shown are older. The period costumes are by no means only "Colonial"; the name is misleading in this sense, but I have retained it because it has been in popular currency since the 1940's. In fact, the fad for Early American everything—furniture, knick knacks, house design, etc.—began in the 1920's, along with the Dutch craze. Patterns showing figures in foreign costume and those showing odd or unconventional dress I have called Dutch Dolls. In practice, these categories cross and overlap constantly. My divisions can be regarded as artificial, and yet quilters may find the rough classification useful.

The designs are given in one, two, or three sizes. The more elaborate patterns are given in larger sizes and the simpler examples in smaller sizes; but a design that will fit on a 12-inch square block is given with most patterns in this volume. This means that you can either make a quilt from one of the patterns or choose as many of the patterns as you like to make a Sunbonnet Sampler quilt. The design classification may help you make a selection for such a quilt.

You will find that the Sunbonnet children tend to be younger figures and the Colonial Ladies tend to be older figures. While most of the figures in these patterns are worked in appliqué, many can be embroidered (either totally or in part), and there is even one pieced pattern. Suggestions for materials, colors, and execution of each pattern are given with the pattern. General Directions applicable to all the quilt patterns begin on page 15. It is important that you read the General Directions carefully before beginning work on any of the quilts.

About fifty of the patterns in this book are from my own pattern collection, which has been gathered together over the last thirty years. The remainder are from the pattern collections of friends, including Cuesta Benberry and Mrs. Jeanne Hindman, and from my collection of old quilt books and women's magazines. There are about a dozen patterns designed by me expressly to fill in gaps in the series. These are all marked as original by my signature. I hope all my readers will obtain as much enjoyment from using these patterns as I have received from gathering the patterns and researching their history.

Illustration of children's activities in the typical Victorian style.

Introduction

History and Social Background

For the better part of 100 years, small figures in huge, head-hiding hats have been among the most popular of the quilt pattern types. They were originally designed by illustrators working in the field of commercial art in the last decade of the nineteenth and the first three decades of the twentieth centuries. The designs were quickly adapted into patterns by professional needle art pattern-makers and by quilters designing patterns for their own handiwork.

In almost eighteen months of searching, I have been able to uncover only a few bare facts and some unproven legends about the origins of these Sunbonnet pattern prototypes. Published materials about the history of commercial art and artists is almost nonexistent, except for the biographies of a very few artists who later were deemed to have crossed from commercial art into the realm of fine arts, such as Kate Greenaway, Winslow Homer, and N. C. Wyeth. Available material about any of the other early commercial artists is almost exclusively about male artists who worked for book publishers or the more expensive (for their time) magazines. Those who developed the several styles of large-hatted children were, by contrast, mostly women who worked for the less expensive women's magazines, children's book publishers, and publishers in such minor commercial fields as postcards and greeting cards. A few of these artists signed their work, but many more worked in complete anonymity, drawing salaries for piecework or for working on the office staff of a magazine.

Magazines were developed in the early nineteenth century from eighteenth-century newsletters. Many educated people, living by choice or by chance away from the word-of-mouth news (and gossip) channels of the larger cities, found that news of important events reached them at an unsatisfactorily—even dangerously—slow pace. If someone had a friend in the city who could pass on news by letter about banking events, ship sailings and arrivals, or war, foreign treaty, and peace, then the news might arrive in weeks rather than months. At some point, one of these obliging city gentlemen, perhaps already writing to several country gentlemen, decided he was performing a service which, if placed on a regular monthly or weekly basis and offered for a fee, might bring him a certain profit. From being handwritten and hand-copied for each subscriber, the newsletters eventually grew into a large enough business to employ printing presses by the end of the eighteenth century. As the newsletters became a recognized business, other features were added, such as travel notes, fiction reviews, biographies of interesting notables, and—finally, in the 1780's—fashion notes for the ladies, complete with the first printed Fashion Plates.

Each newsletter might have a mixture of all of the elements listed above, with the different editors giving greater emphasis to one or another of the topics of more interest to his own subscribers. These topics were mostly chosen to appeal to the male reader, who might (except for the fashion articles) pass on by word of mouth those morsels of news he thought fit for the ears of the female members of his household.

An English publisher was the first to print a small magazine[1] or booklet with fashions and other articles of interest to women. The first attempt at a magazine for women in the United

---

[1]Magazine historians seem to feel that the line between the newsletter and the magazine was passed early in the nineteenth century, when some newsletters began to print advertisements among their articles and illustrations.

1b

262. Baking Day.

Picnic Club at 6 12
Maple Ave., Wednesday
July 17. Please bring
dishes. Anna S. Roberts

2b

"SAYING GRACE."   Copyright, 1905, by U. Co., N. Y.

3b

CLEANING   HOUSE

2

1494

SUNDAY.

4b

1492

FRIDAY.

5b

States was published in 1831–32 in Philadelphia. *The Athenaeum* was carefully edited by a male staff to give women the information on art, literature, travel, and fashion that the men thought was proper. To say the very least, it was not a commercial success: it lasted for only twenty-four issues. Several other magazine publishers, understanding that women were hungry for news and amusements and that a really appealing magazine would be very profitable, made several other ventures—which all failed for the same reason.

Then a gentleman publisher, Louis A. Godey (who published a fairly successful general magazine but had failed in several attempts at a ladies' magazine), had a revolutionary thought: A lady editor might know what women would like to read and know how to present it to them in a palatable form. His was the first successful American women's magazine. Mr. Godey interviewed several candidates for the post of Lady Editor and finally chose a widow with five children for the post, reasoning that her responsibilities would prevent frivolity in her approach to the work. Under its Lady Editor, Sarah Josepha Hale, *Godey's Lady's Book* was published for thirty-eight years. In 1873, when it ceased publication, the *Lady's Book* had

1491   COPYRIGHTED 1905 BY ULLMAN MFG.CO.N.Y.

THURSDAY.

pioneered features comprising the full range of interest in modern women's magazines. Sarah Josepha did indeed know what women liked and how to present it to them.

The *Lady's Book* introduced the custom of paying authors and artists for their work. Another innovation introduced by Sarah Josepha was not only to consider but even to publish work submitted by women. The *Lady's Book* went so far as to give women by-lines in their own names; heretofore, most women had taken either a male pen name, as did George Sand and George Eliot, or (together with some of the more modest male authors) an anonymous, classical pen name such as Publicus or Fortunata. This policy of choosing the best writing or artwork available regardless of the sex of the contributor opened these fields of endeavor to women for the first time. Other publishing firms followed suit in growing numbers. It may not be overstating the case to say that if it were not for Sarah Josepha Hale and Louis A. Godey, who was wise enough to give Mrs. Hale free rein, we might never have had the books of Louisa May Alcott, the poetry of Emily Dickinson, or the illustrations of Kate Greenaway. Mary Cassatt might never have found the courage to leave her very proper family in Pittsburgh and journey to Paris to paint with the bohemian Impressionists, and our museums would not glow with her lovely studies of mothers and their children. Rosa Bonheur might have painted her

4

7b.

8b.

WHEN OUR SHIP COMES IN—WE'LL _____

9b.

JUST A LINE OR TWO

5

beloved horses, but they would probably not have graced the parlors and museums of the Western world. All later female artists would have had a harder time realizing their talents if *Godey's Lady's Book* had not been.

Recently I enjoyed completing a "returning student" course at the Fine Arts College of the University of Texas. One of the attitudes prevalent among some of the older male instructors (and some not-so-old, as well) was that women cannot be great artists because they like flowers and babies too much. If my money and time had not been spent learning what these men could teach me, I would have undertaken to give them a course in "The Social History of Female Artists," which they very much needed.

It was not that women could not handle the same subjects undertaken by male artists, but that society (that is, those persons who might buy their work) would not accept such subjects when portrayed by a woman. Male professional artists had to be very successful indeed to be socially acceptable to Victorians and Edwardians. Female professional artists were even less acceptable. In fact, the nineteenth century acknowledged them hardly at all. Their only remotely acceptable subjects were flowers and babies.

Few artists of any era are financially secure enough to ignore the taste and social strictures of the people who might buy their work. It did not help to make Rembrandt's life easier that later generations called him a genius, and in any case, few artists are geniuses. Another fact frequently ignored is that flowers and babies are a human interest, and many successful male artists have also built their careers on these subjects. It is not the subject undertaken but the talent of the artist that makes a masterpiece.

Another common attitude about art that I deplore is that all so-called Fine Art is by nature excellent and all commercial art trash. Talent is needed for both, and finished work in each field ranges in value from excellent to worthless. The true test of any work of art is whether it appeals to a large proportion of the public—both knowledgeable and untrained—and whether or not the appeal of the work lasts beyond the years of its first introduction. Judged by these criteria, the Sunbonnet illustrations of the better designers are far better Art than they have ever been given credit for.

The Artists

To be complete, our story of the Sunbonnet designs must begin with Kate Greenaway, the doyenne of illustrators who draw children and flowers. Kate (Catherine) Greenaway was born on March 17, 1846, in London, England. She studied art at the National Art Training School in the South Kensington Museum, London. Greenaway illustrated her first book, *Infant Amusements, or How to Make a Nursery Happy* by William H. G. Kingston, in 1867. In this work she introduced her soft, semi-caricature style of depicting children, which differed from the idealized realism practiced by earlier illustrators of the Victorian era. (Compare the Victorian style illustration facing page 1, with the copy of Kate Greenaway on page 11.) Miss Greenaway illustrated her last book, *The April Babies Book of Tunes* by Countess Von Arnim, in 1900. She created at least fifty-five illustrated books and countless magazine illustrations during her working life. Much of her work has been reprinted time and again because of the continuing popularity of her "Little People." Greenaway's work inspired most of the "commercial artists" who followed her in the "Flowers and Babies" field of illustration.

The most serious criticism leveled at Kate Greenaway's style is that it is unrealistic and sentimental, a dream vision of childhood. But an artist has an obligation to portray his or her inner vision of the world. To some, that world is clear and concise; to others, it is soft and dreamlike; to still others, the world seems formless. It is the public, those who see and buy an artist's work, that sits in judgment upon that work. People who "only know what they like" continue to demand that Kate Greenaway's world of children and flowers be reprinted decade after decade.

Many embroidery designs on the patches of fine Victorian crazy quilts were copies of Greenaway illustrations. Because these illustrations do not actually fall within the compass of the patterns in this book, I have redrawn the angle of the hat in one of Kate Greenaway's drawings so that I could include it as a pattern (see page 246).

There is some controversy about who was the real creator of the Sunbonnet designs, but it was thought in the 1890's and is accepted by most people today that their originator was Bertha Corbett (she later added her married name of Melchior to her signature). It is said that one day Bertha and a friend were discussing art. The friend maintained that emotions could be displayed only by the features of the human face, while Bertha took the position that the entire body could be used to display emotions without a face being visible. An idea discussed between friends soon bloomed into reality on Bertha's drawing board, as she illustrated *The Sunbonnet Babies*, a book by Eulalia Osgood Grover, published in 1902.

The Sunbonnet Babies was about three little girls, Mollie, May, and Katie, and their animal friends on a farm. Frontispiece illustration 2a (which is a copy of a paper doll) and illustrations 1b and 3b (which show two of Bertha's postcards) are examples of the many Sunbonnet Babies she designed after her book illustrations proved popular. The postcards are undated but postmarked 1907.

That the Babies influenced her art for the remainder of her life is indicated by Bertha Corbett's design for the first Old Dutch Cleanser "Dirt Fighter" trademark, shown on page 14. This design is given on a graph to allow enlargement for other needleworkers who like this design as much as I do. When I was a child, this figure who never showed her face stimulated my imagination: I was always plotting ways to see the face hidden under the bonnet brim or trying to visualize the hidden features. (Peeking Sue on page 89 is a response to my lifelong frustration with the "Dirt Fighter" and her cousins, the Sunbonnets.)

The other illustrator credited by some with the creation of the Sunbonnet designs was a man, Bernhardt Wall. His little people were published at about the same time as those of Bertha Corbett, and without exact documentation, the question must really remain undecided. There are certain stylistic differences between the Sunbonnet designs of the two artists, notably in the bonnets; Mr. Wall's figures also lack aprons. I have found the Overall Boy in the work of Mr. Wall and not in that of Miss Corbett. It may therefore be that they share credit—Bertha for the girls and Bernhardt for the boys.

The difference in design between the work of the two artists allows me to add one new piece to our puzzle. Among the pattern sources for quilters and other needleworkers are the catalogs of several pattern companies that have been in business continuously since before the turn of the last century. One of these, founded in St. Louis, Missouri, in 1806, is the Ladies Art Company. I have a series of their catalogs, the oldest of which in my collection was printed in the first decade of this century, or before 1910. Among the patterns illustrated in these early catalogs are a page and a half of Sunbonnet embroidery patterns. (They were discontinued at least forty years ago, so I have included a set of the "Seven Days of the Week" and two other designs among the patterns in this book. See pages 31 and 56). If Mr. Wall's postcard designs (Nos. 4b, 5b, and 6b, pages 3 and 4; published in 1905) are compared with the copies of the Ladies Art embroidery designs (page 56), it is plain that they are almost exact duplicates. The two other Sunbonnet designs included in my 1910 copy of the Ladies Art catalog, but I copied them directly from embroidery blocks in an old quilt (see page 31).

We have late Victorian-style crazy quilts from about 1900 with either appliqué or embroidery versions of the Sunbonnets. The appliqué patterns seem to be closer to the Bertha Corbett designs than to those of Bernhardt Wall, but I have not discovered any printed patterns of Bertha Corbett designs. To my knowledge, no definite information is available as to whether another artist designed printed patterns following the Corbett or Wall designs; and no direct link between illustration and printed pattern of the kind I've established for Bernhardt

Gin a body meet a body
Comin' through the rye
Gin a body kiss a body
Need a body cry

Every lassie has her laddie
Ne'er a one hae **I**
Yet a' the lads they smile at me
When comin' through the rye

COMPLIMENTS OF

J. O. & G. N. ROWE

WHOLESALE GROCERS

ONEONTA, N.Y.

Our Mr *E. J. loosgron*

will call on you about *April 73rd*

APRIL, 1907

SUN	MON	TUE	WED	THU	FRI	SAT
·	1	2	3	4	5	6
7	8	9	10	11	12	13
14	15	16	17	18	19	20
21	22	23	24	25	26	27
28	29	30				

"Tis always morning somewhere" Longfellow

Easter Greetings

Wall seems available for Bertha Corbett. It may be that book and magazine illustrations were copied directly, or that the Sunbonnet idea was simply passed from quilter to quilter. In any case, remarkably little concrete information has been preserved about commercial art and artists before 1950, a fact that makes it difficult to clarify this problem of the genealogy of the Sunbonnet designs.

Other Sunbonnet Artists

Some of the other artists known to have done at least part of their work in the Sunbonnet idiom were:

Bertha E. Blodgett, 1866–1941.   Postcard 12b is one of the designs drawn by this prolific artist. Her work includes figures with facial features hidden and figures with facial features exposed in the same drawings.

Dorothy Dixon.   This artist's work was published by the Ullman Company, which also published the postcards of Bernhardt Wall. Miss Dixon's work, except for a somewhat harder outline and darker coloring, is so close to the style of Bertha Corbett that it would today risk violating modern copyright laws. No. 2b on page 2 is Miss Dixon's work.

M. Dulk.   I have one charming Christmas Greeting postcard designed by this artist. The design is reproduced as Mary Christmas on page 239.[1]

Another artist named Benjen is known to have produced work of the Sunbonnet type. In this case, unfortunately, I was not even able to obtain a sample.

The remaining six cards and four place cards that illustrate this chapter represent the work of anonymous artists. The place cards appeared with the party planning column in a 1920 *The Delineator* magazine.

One artist whose work influenced the Sunbonnet designs but who did not herself draw Sunbonnet figures was Grace G. Drayton. Grace was born in Philadelphia in 1877. She began illustrating stories for children with plump boys, girls, puppies, and kittens, each of which was given a distinctive name like Dolly Dingle or Kitty Puss. These characters appeared again and again in her work, forming a long, popular series. When Grace Drayton's reputation as an artist was well established, the Campbell Soup Company asked her to design a series of ads that would appeal to both children and adults. Her Campbell Soup Kids were an instant success— and so effective in boosting canned soup sales that they have been used in every Campbell's Soup advertisement for over fifty years.

The Drayton figures are not in themselves adaptable to Sunbonnet designs; it was her characteristic chubby children that influenced the patterns. However, not all of the pattern designers made their figures merely chubby; most of the Little People designed after Dolly Dingle and the Campbell Kids became popular are distinctly fat. It is this style of figure that helps date patterns and ties them to Drayton's work.

Jessie Wilcox Smith was also born in Philadelphia, in 1879. Jessie Smith's children are more natural than the semi-caricatures and full caricatures drawn by Grace Drayton. The figures are not at all adaptable to appliqué and hardly adaptable to embroidery. But the graceful activity of these figures influenced needlewomen to add similar props and motions to their Sunbonnet designs. Thus we can find Sunbonnets going fishing or chasing butterflies rather than just standing in place. Miss Smith's chief claim to fame was having her illustrations on the cover of *Good Housekeeping* magazine for fifteen years straight. Time enough for quilters to know and love her version of childhood.

---

[1]This material on postcards was given to me by Mrs. Barbara R. Andrews, postcard historian and columnist for the *Antique Trader Weekly*. I am grateful to her for her interest in this project.

This is an invitation hearty
For I am going to have a party
And   want you
Its at 3 o'clock on...day next.
And if you can't come I'll sure be vexed
So   just
             do!
Charles Hugh Kenyon

1c

Dorothy

2c

Pam

3c

Jane

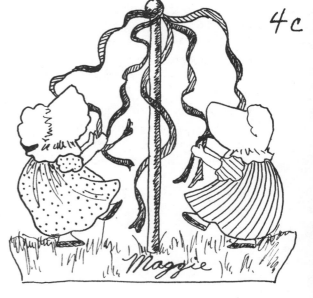

4c

Maggie

1d

1880's

Kate Greenaway

2d

1890's

Bertha Corbett Melchior

3d

1900's

Jessie Wilcox Smith

4d

1920's

Grace G. Drayton

5d

1920's

Modern Priscilla Magazine—Staff Artist

1930's

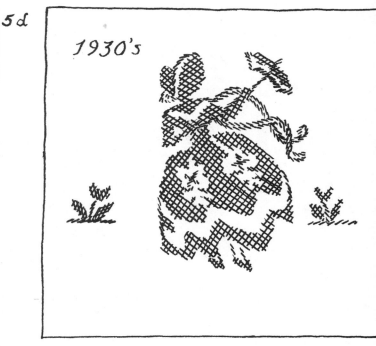

Needlecraft Magazine—Staff Artist

7d

1930's

Needlecraft Magazine—Staff Artist

1940's

Frances Tipton Hunter

Another portrayer of childhood was Frances Tipton Hunter. Frances Hunter was born in Howard, Pennsylvania, in 1896 and educated at the Philadelphia Academy of Fine Arts—as were Grace Drayton and Jessie Smith. She was a great success as a commercial artist; her work appeared regularly in women's magazines and especially on calendars. Frances Hunter's style was a semi-caricature of mischievous, cute kids. Even when her figures were in a still, angelic pose, you knew they had either just finished with mischief or were just about to start some. Her success lasted from the mid 1930's to her death in 1956, and her illustrations still appear in various publications. The attitudes she gave her favorite character, Little Arthur, can be seen in many of the later Overall Boys.

Another artist whose work influenced many people was Queen Hedron, although many of those who enjoyed her work did not know her name. This is another case of an artist's work continuing in demand long after the artist has retired. Queen Hedron used her talent mostly for drawing paper dolls. She met a publisher in the 1920's who thought there would be a demand for her work among children. This was the start of the company that has grown into the Whitman Company, major publishers of paper dolls in the United States for forty years. Mrs. Hedron is not designing her lovely, wide-eyed babies and children any longer, but her work can still be recognized in recent Whitman publications.

We now enter another world, the world of the magazine employee. Free-lance artists signed their work and became nationally known—if not by name, then at least by style. But the artists and designers who worked in the "back room" at the magazine office seldom earned a by-line and they were required to work in so many styles that any one style seldom became familiar to readers. It was anonymous work, however, that was copied most often by quilters, who saw in the fill-in illustrations, the small picture ads, and the needlework or women's-interest column illustrations the basis for many needlework ideas.

In endless sifting of a large collection of womens' magazines, I have been able to find exactly three other names of designers or illustrators who worked on the type of design referred to in this study. By far the greater number of designs were published unsigned. Two of the names on my short list are needlework designer-editors who thus achieved a coveted by-line for their work; the third is one of the back-room artists who did the actual drawings for one of these signed columns and was allowed to sign her drawings.

The first name is that of designer-editor John Then, who worked as the Needlework Department editor of *Woman's World* in 1922. His work is illustrated on the child's apron on page 16 and the two patterns for Lazy Mobcap—Right and Left, page 128.

The second name on our list should be well known to all quilters, as well as to all those interested in dolls. Ruby Short McKim wrote *101 Patchwork Patterns*, which she published herself in 1931. Another publisher took over the book, and this first of all the hardcover quilt pattern books is still in print. What is not so well known is that Mrs. McKim was also one of the designer-editors of the Needlework Department of *Woman's World* magazine in the early 1930's. Her designs in the Sunbonnet style are the patterns I have used for Betty Blue, page 47, and the McKim Dutch Dolls, side and back, pages 149–153. The third name, Agnes Hester Barton, is that of the staff artist who readied Mrs. McKim's designs for publication.

This is little enough to say about the thousands of artists who have earned their living drawing illustrations for the articles, features, and advertisements used in American magazines in the last 150 years. The subject remains a fertile field for investigation, because it is these artists—rather than the much-publicized artists whose work is hung on the walls of museums—that have shaped the tastes of the American public.

One of the fads of the 1920–30 era was an interest in patterns and objects inspired by the folk art and crafts of the Netherlands. The Dutch Doll patterns, both boys and girls, come to us from this era. One of the interesting sidelights of quilting lore is that the name "Dutch Doll" has become the generic name for all the Sunbonnet pattern types—including the Colonial figures—throughout the states of the Deep South.

The Colonial Lady designs were also introduced in the 'twenties and 'thirties, born from a growing interest in the history of the United States which has since continued and flourished. These figures are usually used on quilts meant for someone older than are the designs in the other two categories of patterns.

The 1940's saw the birth of Cowboy and Cowgirl designs. These may have been inspired by President Franklin D. Roosevelt's love of the song "Home on the Range," or perhaps by the popularity of the radio show *The Grand Old Opry*, from Nashville, Tennessee.

By the end of the Depression years of the 1930's and the World War II years of the 1940's, the easy, charming, peaceful world of the Sunbonnet figures seemed out of step with reality. With their sweet simplicity, they disappeared from the pages of magazines, books, and other publications. Only the quilter remembered the "Little People" as ideal for designs to use on the bedding of favorite children. Sunbonnet designs fell out of favor for awhile, but have shown every sign of a renaissance in recent years. The popularity of Holly Hobbie and Strawberry Shortcake figures (which seem to have been influenced by Sunbonnets) suggests that the happy, magic world of the Sunbonnet Babies, Dutch Dolls, and Colonial Ladies (and their boyfriends) is ripe for rediscovery.

Design by Bertha Corbett for the first Old Dutch Cleanser trademark. Taken from an advertisement, page 598 of the October 1908 issue of *The Delineator*.

General Directions

For greater versatility in the use of the following patterns, most have been provided in more than one size (see Index). Patterns are given for 6'', 8'', 9'', 10'', 12'', or 15'' squares, or for 18'' by 22'' quilt centers. In addition to quilt blocks, the smaller sizes can be used on items of clothing (see 1a–6a), pillowcase and sheet sets (8a), or trims for other bedroom or personal items (7, 11a–12a). Design 12a is copied full-size from a 1920 napkin and may be used as a small pattern. The medium-sized patterns are the correct size for use in making stuffed toys or pillows (see 4a, 7a, and 11a). The larger-sized patterns can be made into garment bags, large-sized linen trims, toys, and pillows.

If your kitchen is decorated in the popular 1900 style, curtains, potholders, aprons, towels, and other cloth items (such as tablecloths with matching napkins) could be trimmed with some of your favorite little people. A large Christmas tree could be hung with Sunbonnets in the 6-inch size, and other Christmas items such as tree skirts, table mats, and wall hangings, could feature a mixture of these figures. A sunporch furnished with old-fashioned wicker furniture would look bright and cheery with some of the little Gardeners or Flower Girls and their colorful flowers. Any room that needs a smile will welcome these little people in their big hats.

In addition, craftspersons in other fields might enjoy using the Sunbonnets in their work in woodcarving, plastic or plaster casting, sculpture, pottery, leaded or stained glass, painting, or stencil work. I treasure a plastic bookmark, a plastic refrigerator doll, and a leaded glass piece, all of which were made from patterns published in my magazine columns and sent to me by kind readers.

Choosing a Pattern

Usually, the size of the prospective quilt has been decided before the quilter begins to look for a pattern. The standard sizes are:

Crib, small	3 feet by 4 feet
Crib, large	4 feet by 5 feet
Child's bed	5 feet by 7 feet
Daybed or Cot	4 feet by 6 feet
Twin bed	6 feet by 8 feet
Double bed	7 feet by 8 feet
	or 8 feet by 8 feet
Queen size	9 feet by 8 feet
King size	10 feet by 9 feet
	or 10 feet by 10 feet

The next step is to leaf through the patterns and choose those that appeal to your taste. With these patterns and their sizes in mind, decide on a top design that uses the block size of your pattern. Your pattern should enhance the look of the top design. There are eight different suggestions for both traditional and new ideas in top designs given on pages 18 and 19. The drawings of the eight top designs are given for a little more than one quarter of each entire quilt top; thus, the number of blocks shown should be multiplied by four to arrive at the number

1a

2a

3a

4a

6a

5a

16

ALBUM

7a

8a

9a

10a

11a

12a

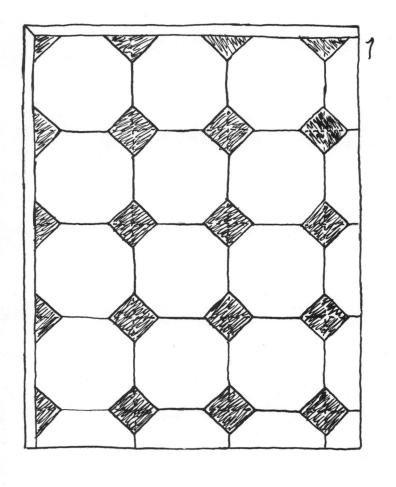

1

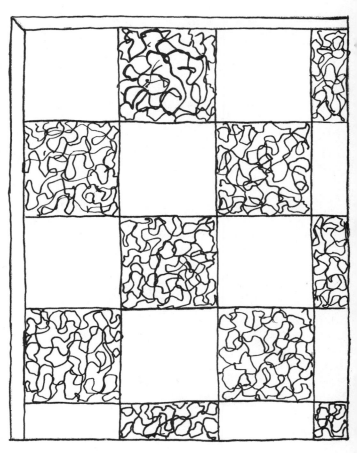

3

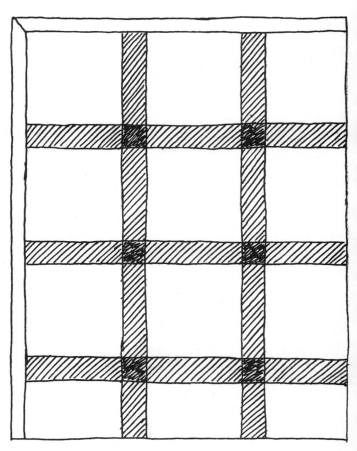

18

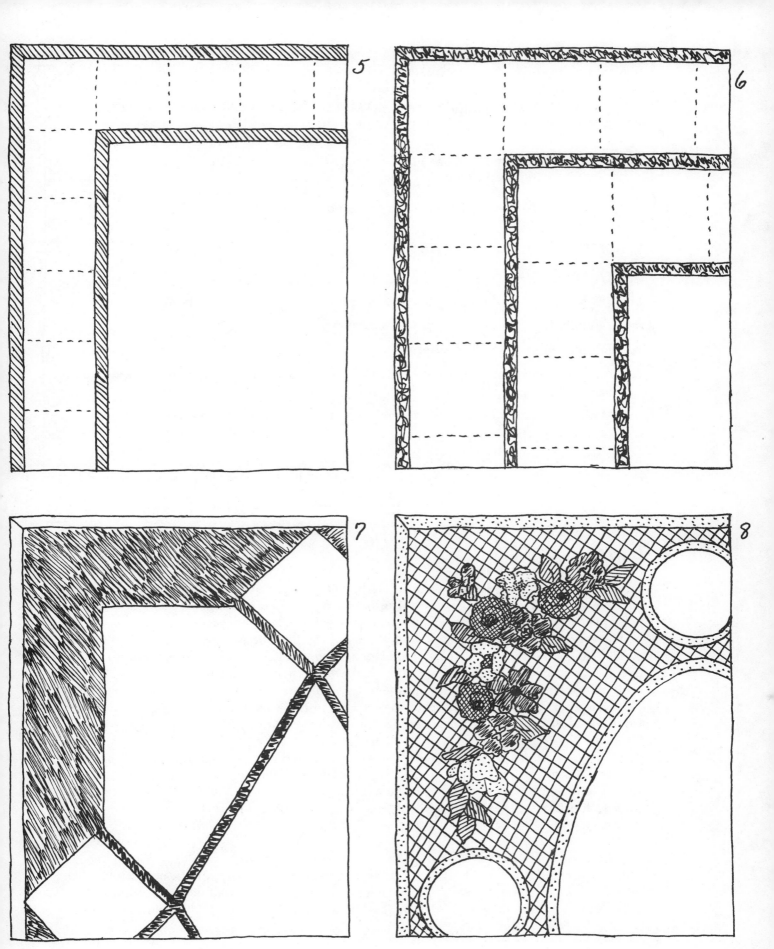

needed for the entire quilt top. Remember that any pattern placed on the diagonal of a block (see top design 3) will fit on a square as much as 2 inches smaller than will be needed if the same pattern is used straight on a block. Thus a pattern marked as for a 12-inch square block will fit on a 10-inch square block if placed on the diagonal.

> NOTE: One of the most important rules of quilt making is always to try a pattern by cutting out and sewing together one trial block to test that the pattern is accurate and that you understand the directions before cutting out the remainder of your material.

Cutting Your Patterns

To begin work on your quilt, you will need cutting patterns. The patterns in this book are all given in finished size—this means that the patterns do *not* have the seam allowance included.

a.   Carefully trace off the patterns on tissue paper.

b.   Cut out the tissue paper patterns.

c.   Trace the tissue paper patterns onto cardboard, taking care to keep them as accurate as possible.

d.   Mark the name of the pattern and piece number on each pattern piece.

> NOTE: Cardboard wears down with use. Cut at least three sets of patterns so that you can change to a fresh pattern when the one you are using becomes worn.

Cutting the Cloth

Lay the pattern on the correct color of cloth. Place it in a corner, ¼-inch from each edge (*excluding the selvage edge*). Draw a firm pencil line around the edge of each pattern. For appliqué patterns, mark the pencil lines on the face of the cloth. For pieced patterns, mark the pencil lines on the wrong side of the cloth. This is so that the penciled lines will be on the correct side of the cloth to serve as a guide for sewing. On light-colored cloth, use a No. 2 soft pencil. For dark colors, use a white conté pencil, which can be bought at any art supply store. A chalk pencil can be used, but the lines you draw will become faint and even disappear in a relatively short time. Move the pattern ½-inch and trace the outline of the pattern again. Continue until all of the patterns needing that particular material have been traced at ½-inch intervals.

   Cut the cloth between the traced lines so that ¼-inch is left on the edge of each piece of cloth to allow for the seam. Make an effort to be accurate about the ¼-inch seam allowance. Be very sure to add the seam allowance when you are cutting your quilt blocks, too. A 12-inch-square, finished-size quilt block should be cut 12½ inches square to keep ¼-inch seam allowance on all four sides.

   In making patterns it is often impossible to print the full size of a very large pattern piece. This is true of all patterns, whether meant for dressmaking, furniture, quilts, or whatever. To indicate that a piece with two identical sides can be cut from a half-pattern, a dotted line indicates the center of the piece. To use this kind of pattern on cloth, fold the unused cloth in half. Place the dotted line of the pattern along the fold and cut out the pattern as if the cloth were not folded. When the cut-out cloth is opened the piece will be complete. If two sides of the pattern have dotted lines, the cloth must be folded in half lengthwise and then across the width, with the pattern placed in the corner so the dotted lines are on the two folds. Cut. This will give a piece with four identical corners, four times the size of the pattern piece. Follow all the other directions for marking and cutting a pattern when using patterns with dotted lines.

Making an Appliqué Quilt Block

Assemble all of the cut cloth pieces needed to make one complete block.

Lay the background square to one side.

Ready the appliqué pieces by clipping excess material in the seam allowance away from all points. Then clip the seam allowance nearly to the penciled line on all curves (see the top diagram on page 22). This will allow you to turn the seam allowance under smoothly all the way around.

Baste the seam allowance under on all of the pieces.

a.   Pin all of the appliqué pieces to the background cloth and make sure they are in the correct place, ready for sewing. Pieces that must touch should touch all along the finished side seams.

b.   Start the needle from the back and make a blind stitch (see diagrams on page 22). To make a blind stitch, put your needle through both the background cloth and the exact edge of the appliqué piece, as near to being in the fold as you can manage. Put the needle back down through the background material right beside the place where your needle came out through the appliqué piece. The next stitch should be ¼-inch or less from the first stitch. When done correctly and neatly a blind stitch hardly shows at all.

> NOTE: Do not sew the appliqué to the background cloth with em-
> broidery stitches without first sewing the edges down with the blind
> stitch. This is very important because embroidery floss is no longer
> made with a tight twist, so it is not as strong as thread. It will wear out
> very fast and leave your appliqué pieces loose to ravel or tear away
> from the quilting stitches or background material.

Embroidery Stitches

The elaborate needlework of the Victorian era became unfashionable by the 1890's and the vast number of stitches once used by needleworkers was reduced to a simple few. Fashion's pendulum began to swing back in the late 1950's, and needleworkers now again take pleasure in being able to make hundreds of different stitches. The patterns in this book will look well when done with any of your favorite stitches. In addition to fancy outline stitches, you might try surface-filling stitches and surface-powdering stitches to cover the large blank spaces in these patterns. However, some of my readers will take pleasure in recreating these patterns in the original limited range of stitches, whether all embroidery stitches or appliqué with embroidery is the method of execution used.

The outline stitches that were popular when Sunbonnet designs were first widely used in needlework were the *stem stitch*, the *split stitch*, and (used to a lesser extent) the *back stitch*. The *French knot* was a very popular stitch used for dots, flower centers, and buds—either

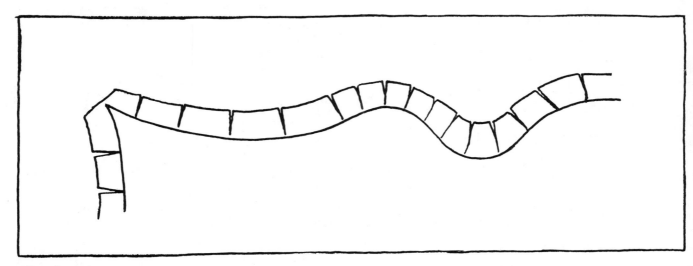

Clipped curves.

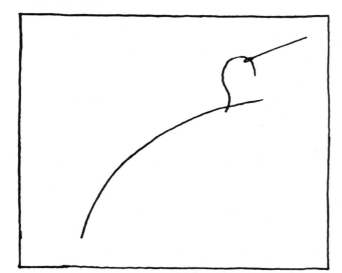

Blind stitch I.

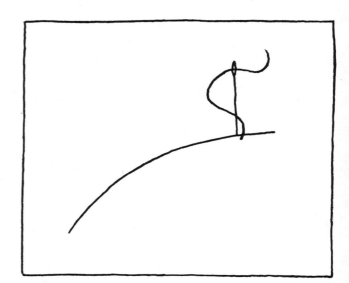

Blind stitch II.

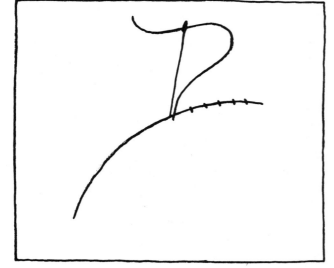

Blind stitch III.

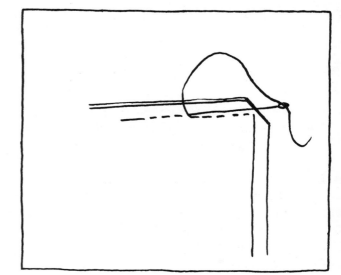

Piecing.

singly or in clusters. *Detached chain, bird's eye,* and *daisy petal* are all names for the same stitch shown in diagram 5. The last stitch diagramed is the *long and short* or *Kensington stitch,* which was used for covering areas solidly. This stitch was more popular than the similar *satin stitch* because larger areas could be covered without having to use stitches long enough to snag easily. For outlining pieced or appliqué patches, the *blanket* or *buttonhole stitch* and some of the plainer *feather stitches* were used. For real period-look needlework the stitches must be simple.

REMINDER: Do not use the buttonhole or feather stitches in embroidery floss to fasten down appliqué patches without first appliquéing the patches with blind stitches or hemstitches in sewing thread. Some quilters have mistakenly decided that the rules for machine appliqué (see page 27) also apply to handwork; they do not. If hand-sewn appliqué patches are not sewn down with regular thread first, they will be lost when the embroidery floss wears through.

1. Stem Stitch

Stem stitches are an overlapping line of stitches that look rather like a line of overlapping shingles on the roofline of a house. To make this stitch, sew a single stitch starting from the back of the material at one end of the pattern line. This stitch should be ⅜-inch long or less (A). Place the needle through the material at the end of this stitch and return the point of the needle to the surface ⅛-inch back alongside the first stitch (B). Continue in this manner until the pattern line has been covered (C).

2. Split Stitch

This stitch must be made with embroidery floss with an even number of strands: 4, 6, or 8. Make the first stitch at one end of the pattern line ⅜-inch or less in length (D). Bring the point of the needle back to the surface of the material, ⅛-inch less than the length of the first stitch (E). Place the point of the needle ⅛-inch inside the near end of the first stitch, with an equal number of floss strands on each side of the needle point (F). Continue in this manner until the pattern line has been covered (G).

3. Back Stitch

The back stitch is a simplified form of the split stitch. When done correctly it looks like a string of beads. Make the first stitch on the front of the material, ⅜-inch or less in length, at one end of the pattern line (H). Move the point of the needle to a place on the back of the material exactly the same distance ahead as the length of the first stitch; pull the needle through and reinsert it back at the point where the first stitch ended (I). Continue in this manner until the entire pattern line is covered (J).

4. French Knot

Start the stitch by bringing the thread through the material from the back to the front at the point where the pattern indicates a knot is needed. Lay the needle on the material next to the end of the thread (K). Wind the floss around the needle two or three times, depending on the size of the knot needed (L). Place the point of the needle back through the material near but *not* at the place where the thread first emerged (M). Hold the three loops in place with your thumbnail so the loops will not loosen or tighten as the thread is pulled through them (N). A small back stitch on the back of the material will insure that the knot is held firmly when finished.

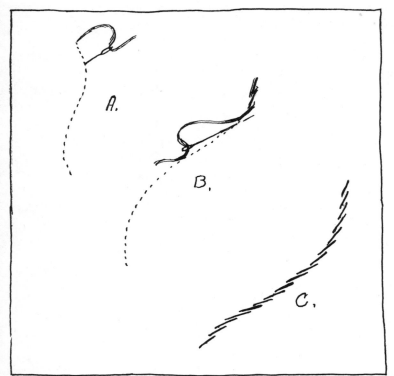

1. Stem stitch

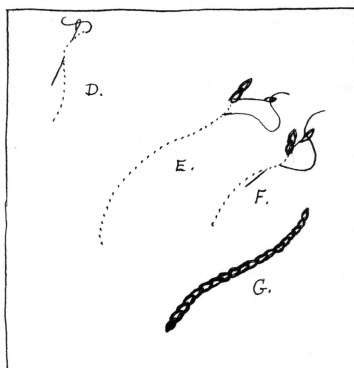

2. Split stitch

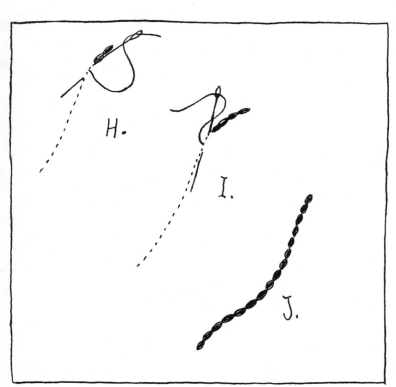

3. Back stitch

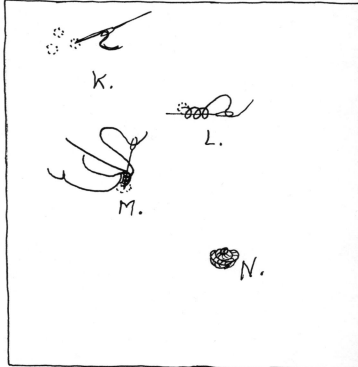

4. French knot

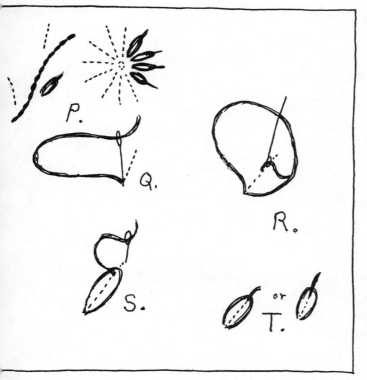

5. Daisy stitch

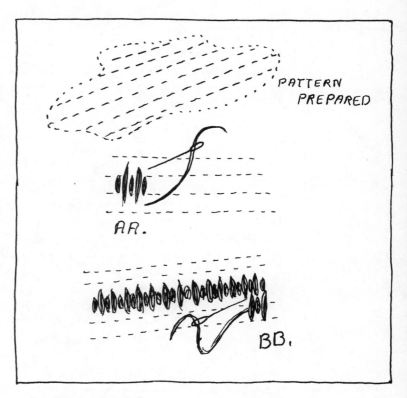

1. free edging W.

2. inner edging

U. V.

6. Buttonhole stitch

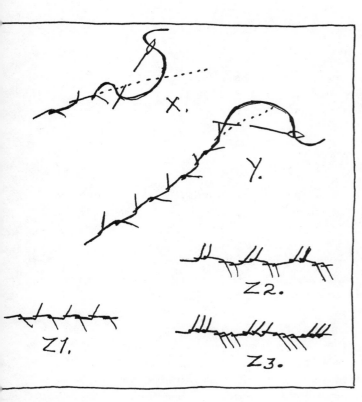

X.

Y.

Z1.

Z2.

Z3.

7. Feather stitch

PATTERN PREPARED

AR.

BB.

8. Kensington stitch

25

5. Daisy Stitch

This stitch was used for small leaves on either side of rows of stem stitches; it was also used in circles as flower petals. The pattern illustrating this stitch is shown in diagram P. To make the stitch, bring the thread through the material from the back to the front at the inner end of a pattern line; form a loop of thread (Q). Put the point of the needle back through the material in the same place and return it to the surface at the other end of the pattern line (R). Catch the loop of thread with a tiny back stitch (S). A variation of this stitch has a long rather than a tiny back stitch, and the loop occupies only three quarters or less of the length of the pattern line (T).

6. Buttonhole Stitch

This stitch is only used on edges—either free edges or the edges of material applied to background material. If used on free edges as an alternate to binding material, the stitches must be made very close together to protect the edges with the thread of the stitches. When used as a decorative internal stitch, the individual stitches may be slightly separated by as much as ¼-inch.

Pull the thread through the material from the back to the front. Loop the thread over a finger of your opposite hand (U). Place the needle through the material in a stitch beside the first stitch; catch the loop under the point of the needle and pull it tight but not taut (V). Repeat until the edge is covered (W).

7. Feather Stitch

This is merely a decorative edging for internal seams of either pieced or appliquéd work. It is made in a manner similar to that used for the blanket stitch, but the stitches are shorter, slanted, and made on *both* sides of the center line. For this stitch, review items (U) and (V) in both the diagram and the written directions for 6. Make the side stitch about ⅛-inch long and slant it toward the center line (X). The next stitch is the same, except that it is made on the other side of the center line (Y). This stitch may be made with one, two, or three side "feathers" in groups on either side of the center line (/1, /2, /3).

8. Kensington Stitch

To fill in areas with solid embroidery, this is a useful as well as an ornamental stitch. Before embroidering a finished piece using this method, it would be well to practice first, because the best results with this stitch are obtained when the two sizes of stitches are continually even in length and placement. The longer stitch should be ½-inch long and the smaller stitch about ¼-inch long (or lengths in relative scale for larger or smaller work).

The area to be embroidered can be lined off with pencil lines ¼-inch apart (or the width of the smaller stitch's length). Make a short stitch between two of the lines. Then place the needle through the material from the back at a place halfway between the two lines below those used by the first stitch. This second stitch should reach to a point halfway between the two lines above the first stitch (AA). Place another short stitch alongside the long stitch. Continue until the first line of stitches reaches the end of the area to be covered. Make a second line of stitches, placing a short stitch below a long one and vice versa (BB). Continue reversing the direction of the work for each line until the area is completely covered. This stitch is easiest when the first line is worked across the center of the area halfway between the upper and lower edges, and finished above and then below this first line.

Machine Appliqué

There are two methods of appliquéing with a sewing machine. The method used depends on the type of sewing machine available to the quilter. Method 1 is used by quilters using a straight-needle machine, and Method 2 should be used on a slant-needle machine.

Method 1: Cut the appliqué patches with ¼-inch-wide seam allowances on all sides. Turn this seam allowance under and baste it in place. To turn the seam allowance easily and smoothly, clip the edges where necessary to make it lay smooth. Sew the patch to the background material with a line of stitches ⅛-inch or closer to the folded edge. Finish as with hand sewing.

Method 2: Cut the appliqué patches on the sewing line *without* seam allowances. Set the machine to make stitches ¼- or ⅜-inch long and as close together as the dial will allow. Cover all of the edges of the patch with stitches close enough together to look like satin-stitch embroidery. This is necessary to keep the edges of the patch from wearing or raveling with use.

Putting Your Top Together

When all of the blocks (plain and either pieced or appliquéd) are finished, lay them out in order on a large surface or floor. Place each block, lattice strip, and border in its position. Now stand back and look at the results. If you do not like something, now is the time to change it—especially in scrap quilts. Now is the time to check whether several blocks of the same color are too close together. Study the arrangement carefully, and rearrange until you are satisfied with the quilt top.

Starting with the top left-hand corner, take up each row of blocks with the left block on top. Pin a paper with the number of the row on each row of blocks. Carefully sew each block of the first row together. When you have sewn all of the blocks together into individual rows, sew the rows together in numerical order. Be sure each corner is exactly together with the corners of the next row.

Marking Your Quilt

There are two ways of marking a quilt. Most patterns can be traced onto the cloth with a No. 2 (soft) pencil. For hard or complicated patterns you may obtain an iron-on pencil from most needlework supply houses.

To mark the entire quilt top with one pattern in the old-fashioned way (where fans, shells, diamonds, or squares are used in an all-over design), reverse the quilt in the frame and mark the pattern on the backing of the quilt so the pattern on the top does not confuse you.

If you decide to use one of the fancy patterns in the clear areas of the quilt, you must outline the appliqué or all the pieces in the pieced sections. Fit your fancy patterns into the exact center of the clear spaces and make sure they are the correct size to fill the space without crowding it.

Read the section on making a quilt-top pattern before you make your quilting patterns. A quilting pattern is made exactly like a quilt top pattern.

To use an iron-on pencil, trace the pattern onto tissue paper with a regular pencil; then retrace the pattern with the iron-on pencil. Reverse your paper pattern and, using a slightly hot iron, transfer the pattern to the cloth. After you have finished quilting the quilt and have bound the edges, you will have to wash the quilt to remove the water-soluble, iron-on pencil markings. If you have used Dacron as your quilt filler, washing the quilt will not hurt its looks. It will still look brand-new after washing.

Putting Your Quilt in the Frame

There are three basic types of frames for quilting.

1. The large room-size frame is made with four 1''-by-2'' boards about 10 feet long (12 feet long for king-size quilts). They may be held in position by four C clamps—one for each corner of the frame. The frame may be held up by four chairs, four stands, small wooden horses, or by fastening it to four pulleys attached to the ceiling. However your frame is set up, two of the boards must be 2 feet longer than the side measurement of your quilt, and the other two boards must be 2 feet longer than the length of your quilt.

2. A table-size frame is made with two 10-foot-long dowels and two side stands which hold the dowels about 2 feet apart. If you do not have an entire large room to devote to a quilting frame, this table frame is the next-best solution.

3. A lap frame is a large, oval, wooden hoop much like a very large embroidery hoop. If you wish to carry your quilting with you from room to room or even away from your home, a lap frame is the solution.

To fix a regular frame or a table frame for quilting, there is some work to be done. Take an old, worn-out sheet and tear it across the center width. Wrap one piece of the cloth around each of the two end boards of the regular frame or around each dowel of the table frame. One edge of the cloth can be fastened to the board by thumbtacks. Then wrap the material loosely around the board and sew the outer edge down. This is so that the quilt can be attached to the frame. If you use tacks to attach the quilt, it could tear.

To place the quilt in the regular or table frame, baste one end of the backing to one of the end boards wrapped with the sheet. Place the filler smoothly on this backing. Spread the top of the quilt over the filler smoothly and stretch all three layers taut. On the regular frame, pin holding strips to the sides of the quilt, loop them around the side boards, and pin again to the quilt (see diagram 2, page 29). This will hold the quilt stretched along the two sides. On the table frame, roll the dowel and quilt smoothly. When just enough of the end of the quilt is left to stretch the width of the table, baste the other end to the front dowel.

After basting the end of the quilt to the front of the regular frame, make sure the four boards are stretched taut and all four corners are fastened securely. Baste the top and filler around the edges to the backing.

To fix a quilt for quilting in a lap frame, lay the backing on the floor or a very large table and spread the filler and top smoothly over it. Baste all the way around the outside of the top, through all three layers. Then baste the width and length of the quilt with lines of stitches about 6 inches apart. Be sure to baste the entire quilt so the three layers cannot slide out of position. Then place the hoop in the center of the quilt and begin quilting. When the area within the hoop has been filled, move the hoop to an adjoining area and continue.

Binding Your Quilt

Cut strips of cloth 1½ inches wide and sew them to the front edge of your quilt ¼-inch from the edge. If your quilt has rounded or projecting edges, such as those on the Double Wedding Ring quilt, cut these strips on the bias. Fold the strip over the raw edge of the quilt and fold ¼-inch of the strip under. Sew this to the back edge of the quilt with a blind stitch.

Do not use a sewing machine to sew the quilt binding. It is the first place that wears on a quilt and you will need to replace this binding about every fifteen years if your quilt is in regular use.

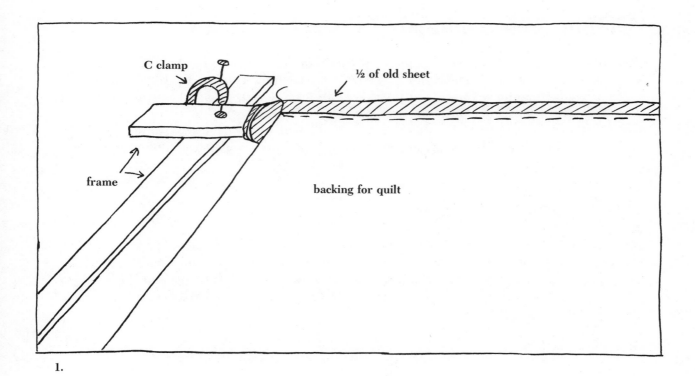

C clamp

½ of old sheet

frame

backing for quilt

1.

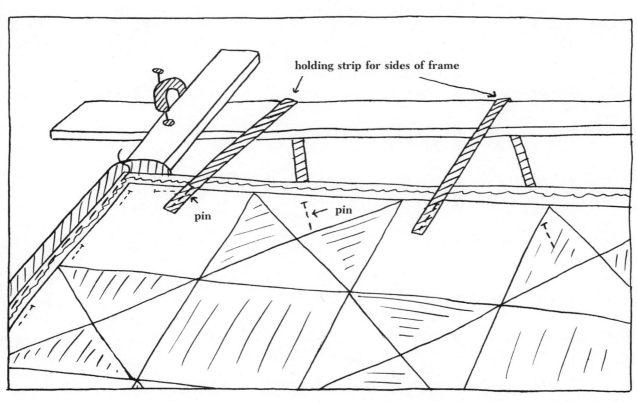

holding strip for sides of frame

pin

pin

2.

Washing Your Quilt*

Do not dry-clean any but the oldest and most fragile quilts. Wash the quilt in warm water and mild detergent in a washing machine. It will not hurt the quilt. Tumble-dry in a dryer with the setting on *warm*. Remove the quilt just before it is entirely dry; the greatest danger to the life of a quilt is overdrying the cloth, which weakens it.

　　If you do not have access to a dryer, hang the quilt between two lines so it forms a U. *Never use an iron on a quilt*. The beauty of a quilt is in the puffiness, which ironing can completely destroy.

Maintaining Your Quilt

Quilts should be treated just like any fine linens. Wash them when they become soiled or dusty. A most important point is never to fold a quilt twice on the same fold marks; a quilt can wear badly along fold marks. If the quilt is folded in fourths the first time, it should be folded in thirds the next time. Remember, a quilt should last anywhere from 25 to 300 years, according to the care taken of it.

---

*These instructions do not apply to quilts in which certain fine fabrics like velvet have been used. Quilts made with fine fabrics should be cared for the same way you would care for clothing made of these materials. If you are in doubt, consult a reputable dry-cleaner, preferably one who specializes in antique quilts and clothing.

6-in. figure

Sunbonnet Babies

Kissing Sunbonnets and Sledding Sunbonnets—1907

These charming patterns were designed by Bernhardt Wall and included in a 1910 *Ladies Art* needlework catalog. They are given in the exact size of the original designs I copied from old embroidered quilt blocks. The designs will fit on 6-inch square blocks.

The original embroidery was done in stem stitch, in turkey-red pearl cotton embroidery thread. This thread is still available from some weaving materials catalogs if you wish to make a period reconstruction quilt. The originals were embroidered in one color but it would also look well in several colors.

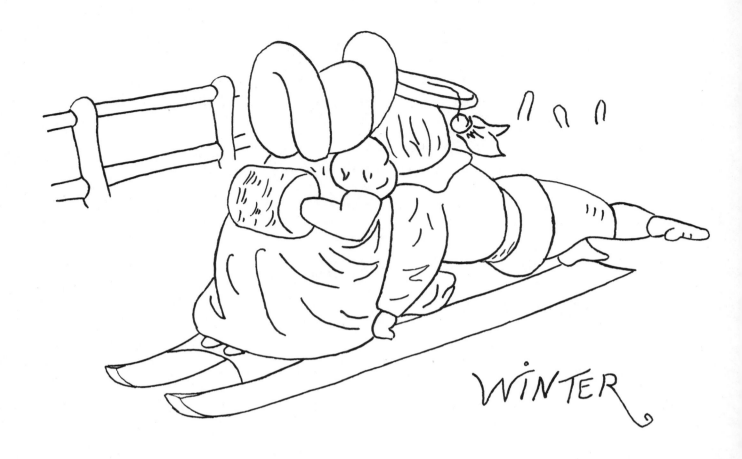

Sledding Sunbonnets

Seesaw Babies—1946

This cute design was one of a set of embroidery patterns that was to be used to decorate a nursery. My scrap of the original envelope is very worn, so much information is lost; but I thought this pattern was cute enough for a quilt block. You can either embroider the pattern on a 15-inch block or do it in appliqué—the pieces are large enough to make cutting patterns from.

The dot-dash outline is the seesaw balance. Place this piece about 1 inch from the lower edge in the middle of the block, feet even with the lower edge. Place the board (dotted line) with the small circle on the small circle of the balance and on the same angle as is shown in dot-dash lines at the top of the balance. The girl should be placed at the right end of the board and the boy at the left end. See the dash lines on the board pattern showing the girl's feet and the boy's hand for correct placement.

Be accurate in placing the pieces.

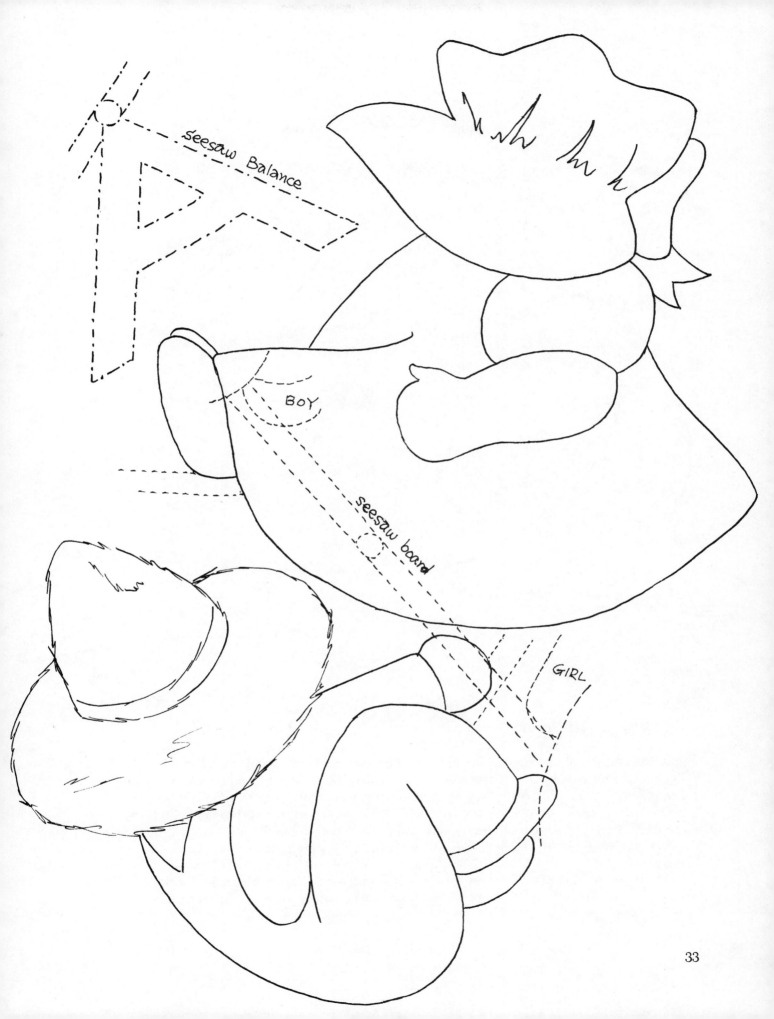

seesaw Balance

BOY

seesaw board

GIRL

33

8-inch block

Praying Sunbonnets—1982

These two little people are shown giving thanks. I have given them a small cross, but any other religious symbol could be substituted. The individual 6-inch figures are appropriate for clothing, curtains, or pillowcases as well as for a baby quilt. Together, the figures require an 8-inch block. If each figure were appliquéd to an 8-inch square block, the cross could be embroidered on a 3-inch lattice square and set between the two appliquéd blocks. (See top design No. 4, page 18). The large figures will fit on a 12-inch square block if used together on one block.

The sections marked with a *b* are for the boy, and those marked with a *g* are for the girl. You may cut out the ruffle on the front of the girl's bonnet brim, or you might fit a ruffled length of lace to the brim.

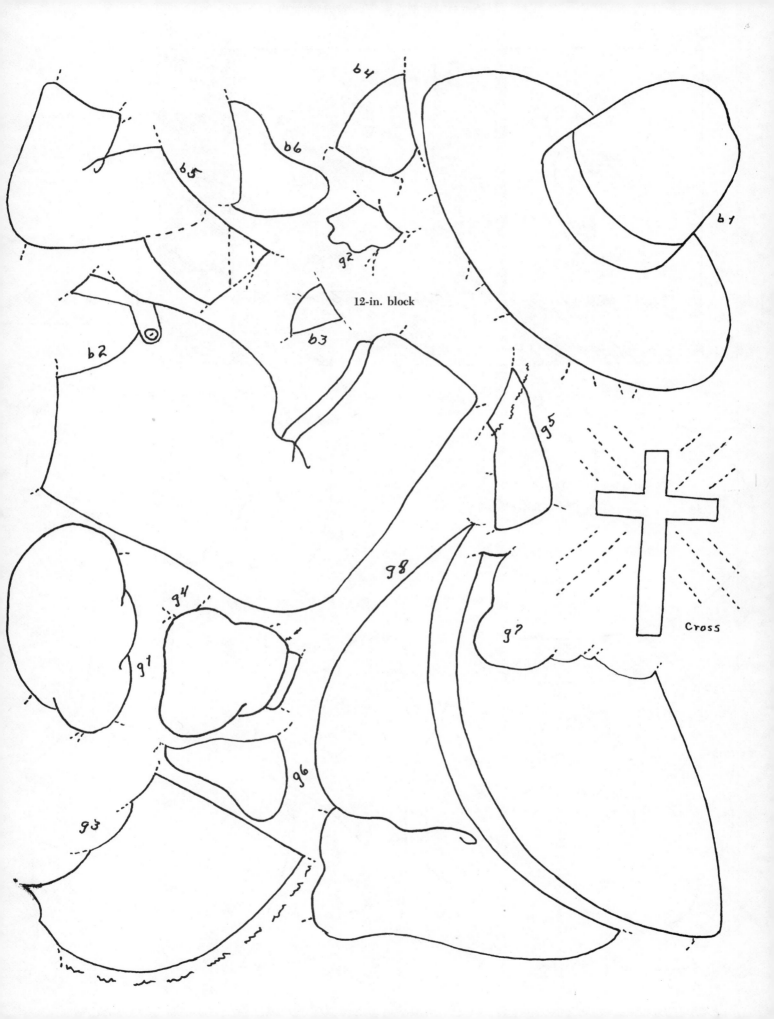

b4

b6

b5

b1

g2

b2

12-in. block

b3

g5

g8

g4

g1

g7

Cross

g6

g3

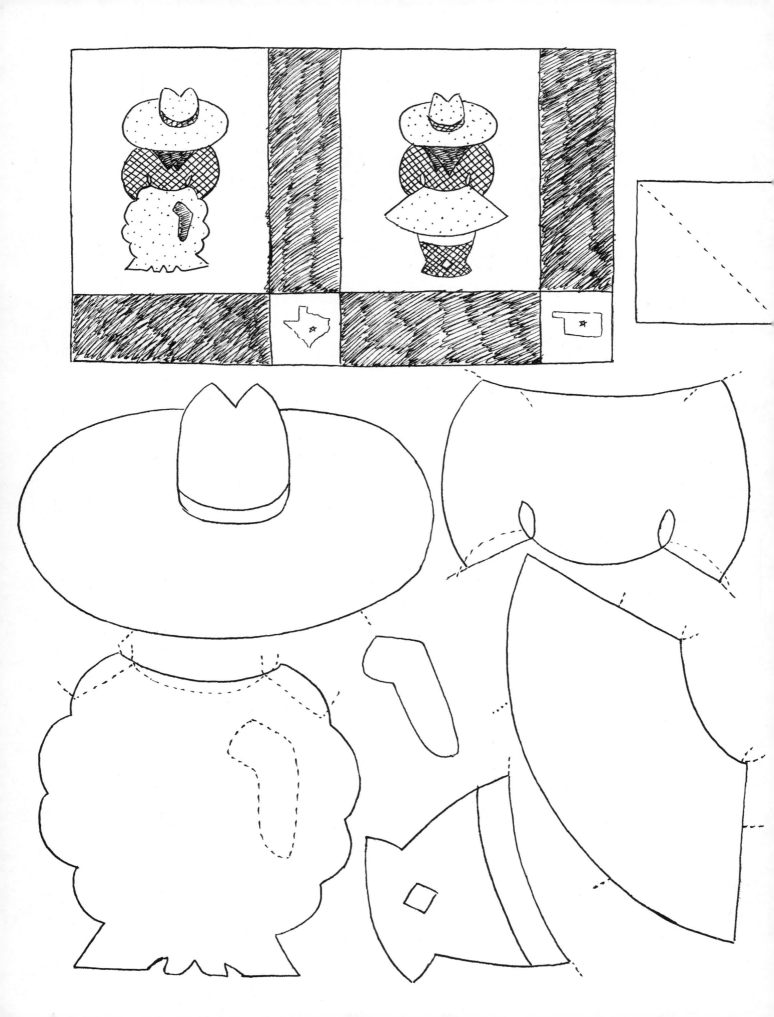

Cowboy and Cowgirl—1960

In 1967 I held a contest for children's quilt patterns for the readers of my *Popular Needlework* magazine column. These two little people were one of the entries. They are to be used on one block each, and have been drawn for 9-inch and 12-inch square blocks. The 9-inch block pattern will fit on a 6-inch block if placed diagonally.

    I have drawn the figures for either embroidery or appliqué in both sizes. The interesting feature is the neckerchief attached to the lower edge of each hat. Fold the square on the dotted line and sew it to the lower edge of the hat so the bottom corners of the neckerchief are free.

    I have drawn a lattice design with state map outlines in the corner squares. These can be obtained in several sizes from maps or atlas pages.

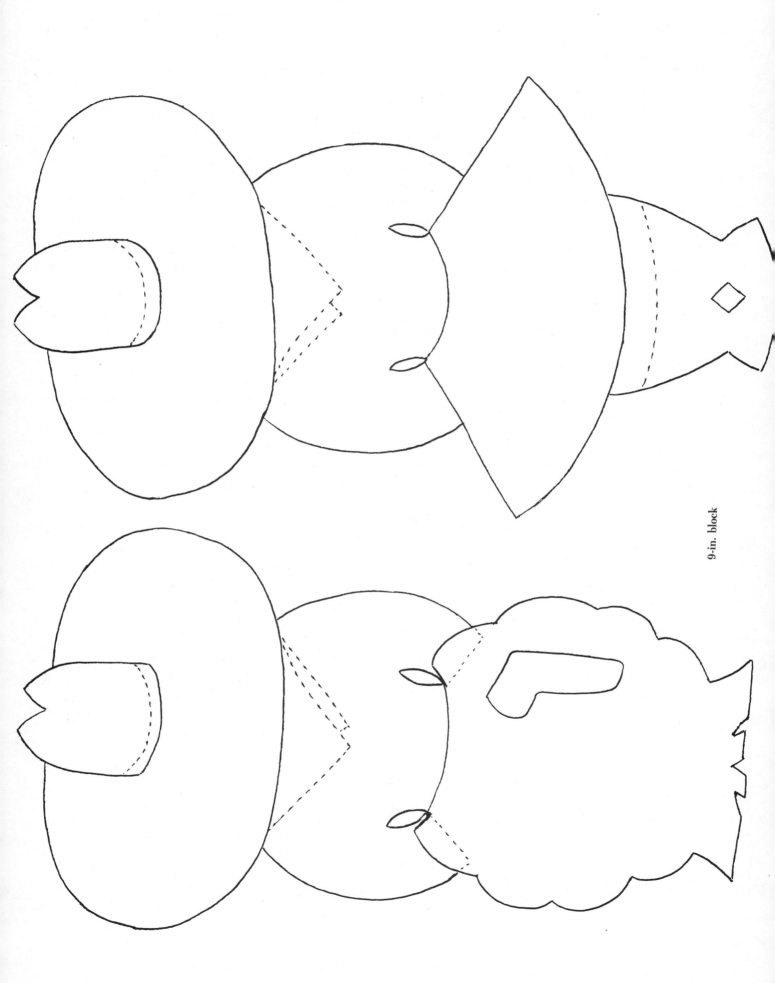

9-in. block

12-in. block

39

12-in. block

40

12-in. block

12-in. block

42

Umbrella Sue—1966

My favorite quilt magazine is not being published any longer. It was *Aunt Kate's Quilting Bee*, and I treasure all the issues in my library. This pattern was sent to the magazine by a reader who named the little figure for her daughter. It seems to me that this design deserves a wider publication, so I have included it for your enjoyment.

The figure can be embroidered or appliquéd in either size. The smaller size is for a 10-inch square and the larger for a 12-inch square block. I have drawn the larger figure as if for embroidery and the smaller figure showing the pieces necessary for appliqué.

10-in. block

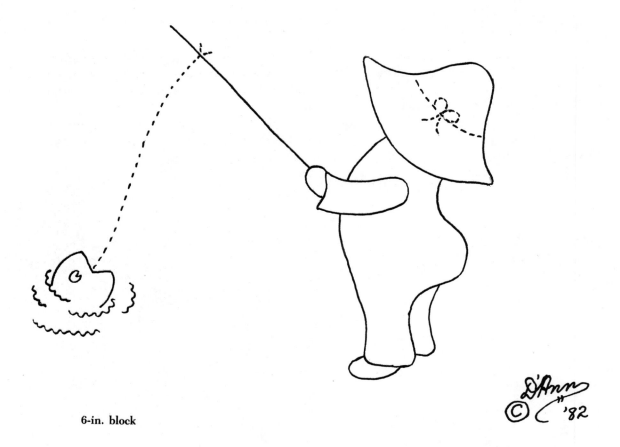

6-in. block

44

Baby Fisherman—1982

This pattern was not planned for. When I drew the clothing on page 16, the little fisherman seemed to spring out of my pencil onto the blouse (see 5d). When I thought about it, I knew some of my readers would want to make him—so I drew him as a pattern exactly as he first appeared.

Patterns are given for 6-inch, 9-inch, and 12-inch square blocks. Thus, these three sizes can be fitted to clothing for very small or larger children. They are, of course, also suitable for quilts and other items. The figure may be either embroidered or appliquéd. The fishing line, the water, the fish's eye, and the ribbon on the hat should be embroidered, even if the remainder of the figure is appliquéd.

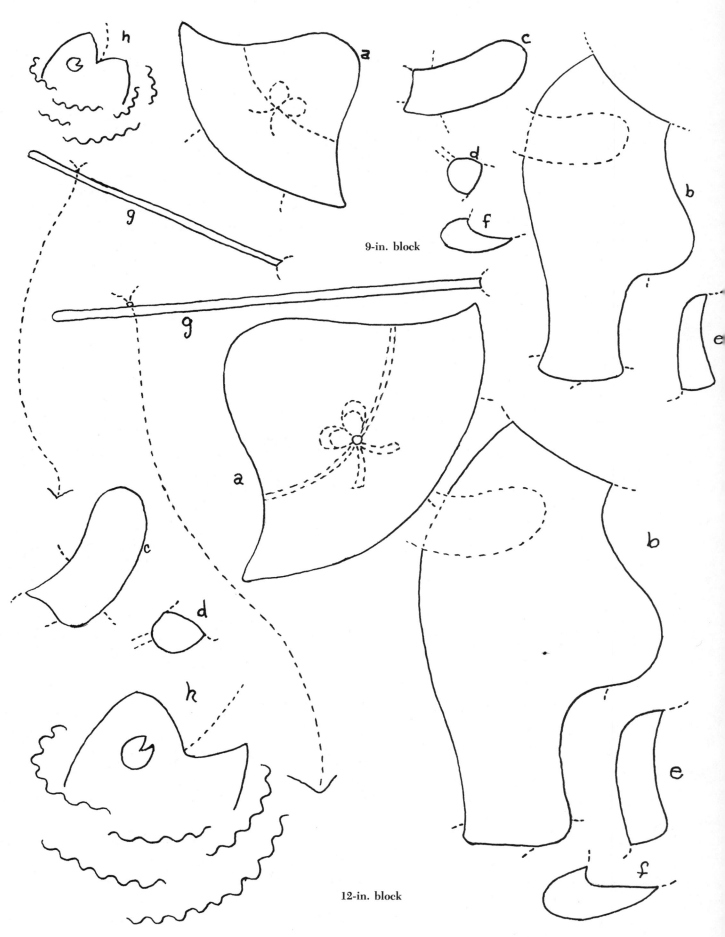

h

a

c

d

f

b

g

9-in. block

e

g

a

c

d

b

h

e

f

12-in. block

46

10-in block

Betty Blue

Betty Blue—1935

This pattern was illustrated in *Woman's World* magazine. Ruby Short McKim designed it at the time she was editor of the Needlework Department.

During this time, a small bed called a youth bed was in use, larger than a crib but smaller than a twin bed. This Sunbonnet design was originally given large enough for the figure to be placed in a simple landscape on a bedspread in the youth-bed size. I have drawn the pattern in more usable sizes, for 10-inch and 12-inch square blocks. It would be fairly easy to enlarge this pattern, however.

The figures are quite simple in outline and can be appliquéd or embroidered, as you wish. Betty's name should be embroidered if embroidery is used. The rhyme for Betty Blue can be embroidered on the quilt top as well:

> Little Betty Blue
> Lost her holiday shoe;
> What shall little Betty do?
>
> Give her another
> To match her other
> And then she'll walk upon two.

12-in. block

Anticipation

50

Anticipation—1940's and Triumph—1982

I am quite sure that the figure I have named Anticipation started out as an illustration in a child's coloring book and was later redrawn as a pattern. It arrived in the mail from a friend quite a few years ago and has been in my collection ever since. When I decided to include this pattern, my mother said, "But he needs a girlfriend." So I redrew the body facing the other way, added a bonnet and basket, and gave her a fish to justify the name of Triumph. The patterns can be embroidered or divided for appliqué. They will each fit on a 12-inch square block.

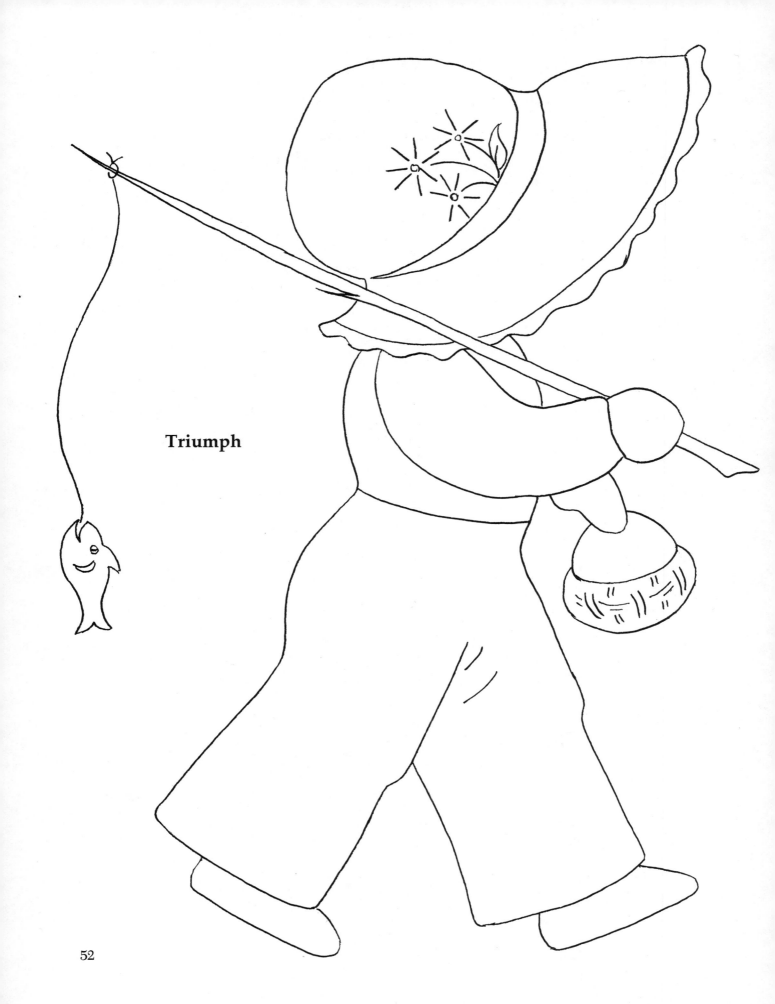

Triumph

52

Good Night

Good Night and Good Morning—1936

Joe Palooka was an old, Depression-era newspaper comic strip. One of the characters in this strip was Dondi—an appealing, large-eyed little newsboy who wore a grown man's cut-down clothing. These two little people belong to the same era. They are drawn for 12-inch square blocks and can be either embroidered or appliquéd, as you prefer.

"Sunday School Picnic," Mennonite quilt, 1932. 84 in. × 82 in. Collection of Nancy Starr.
Photograph courtesy of Thos. K. Woodard, American Antiques and Quilts.

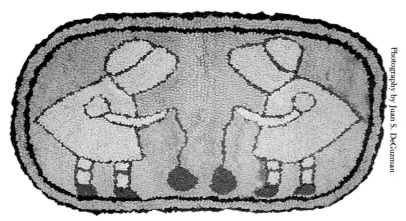

Photography by Juan S. DeGuzman

Oval hooked rug from New England, c. 1920. Collection of Mr. and Mrs. David S. Howe. Courtesy of Made in America Country Antiques and Quilts.

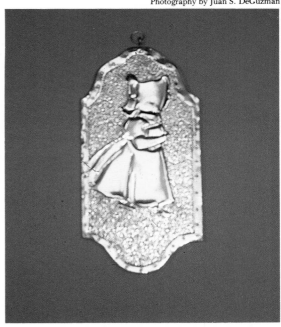

Photography by Juan S. DeGuzman

Brass wall plaque, variation of Seven Days of the Week—Sunday. Probably pre-World War I. Courtesy of Madelyn Larsen.

Embroidered crib coverlet with Sledding Sunbonnets, turkey-red on white, c. 1900's. Author's collection.

Blocks from the author's quilter's catalog, including Sunbonnets Kissing, Baby Fisherman, Springtime Mollie, Seven Days of the Week II—Sunday, Overall Bill, and traditional Sunbonnet Sue; and Katinka (leaded glass).

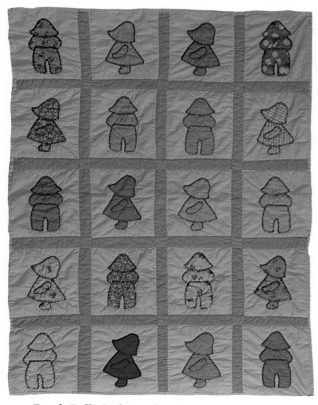

Dutch Dolls Quilt. Made in Texas in 1949 by Betty
Stroud for her daughter Sandra. Collection
of Sandra K. Nodler.

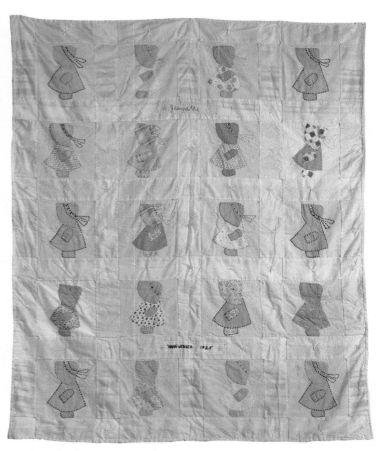

Sunbonnet Sue quilt. Made in 1925 by Nana Webber
of Northhampton, MA, when she was in her eighties.
Reconditioned. Author's collection.

Photograph by Joanne Canestra

Colonial Lady Sunbonnet quilt. Made in 1940 by
Mary Rowley of Hornell, NY. Collection of her niece,
Mrs. Mary Lou Gottschall.

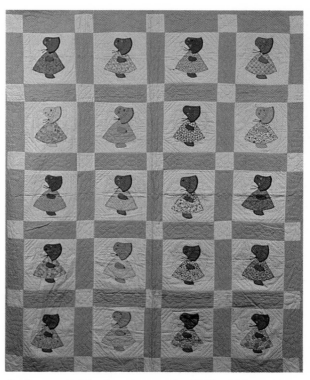

Sunbonnet Babies American quilt, 1920's. 86 in. × 70 in.
The Brooklyn Museum; Gift of Mrs. Margaret S. Bedell.

Sunbonnet Sue double-bed sized quilt. Made by Gypsy Dowling in 1931. Quilted with embroidery floss. Collection of Anita Murphy.

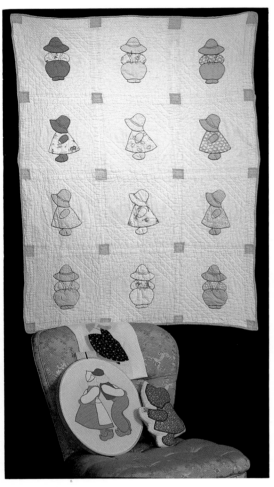

Dutch Boy/Dutch Girl quilt, c. 1930's; collection of Laura Matkin. "Windblown" Colonial Lady made by and in the collection of Bonnie McCoy. Kissing Dutch Dolls made by and in the collection of Diane Herbort. Sunbonnet Doll made by and in the collection of Francine Tapia.

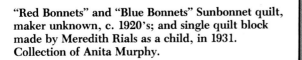

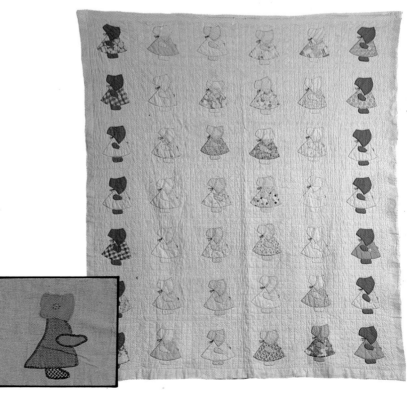

"Red Bonnets" and "Blue Bonnets" Sunbonnet quilt, maker unknown, c. 1920's; and single quilt block made by Meredith Rials as a child, in 1931. Collection of Anita Murphy.

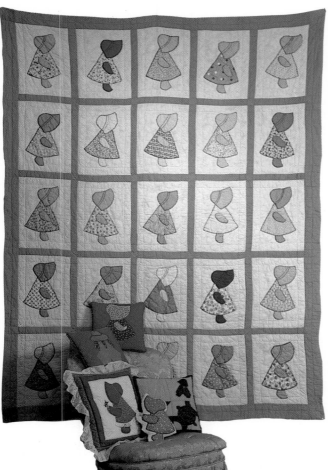

Sunbonnet quilt, made for Mr. Hull Youngblood by his mother, c. 1920s; collection of Mr. and Mrs. Hull Youngblood. Blue Sunbonnet Sue and Overall Bill pillows and four-block blue pillow made by and in the collection of Beverly A. Orbelo. Ruffled Sunbonnet Sue pillow and Sunbonnet stuffed doll made by and in the collection of Francine Tapia.

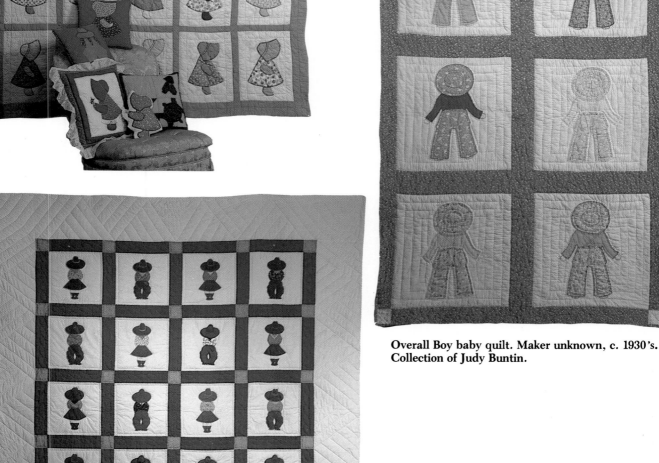

Overall Boy baby quilt. Maker unknown, c. 1930's. Collection of Judy Buntin.

Cowboy and Cowgirl quilt. Designed by Beverly A. Orbelo; made by the Star Quilters of San Antonio, TX.

"Life and Times," wall hanging. 46 in. × 70 in. Designed and made by Anita Murphy in 1980.
Collection of Anita Murphy.

Sunbonnet Sue quilt. Appliqué done in 1935; top pieced and quilted in 1983 by Charlotte Christiansen Bass. Collection of Charlotte Christiansen Bass.

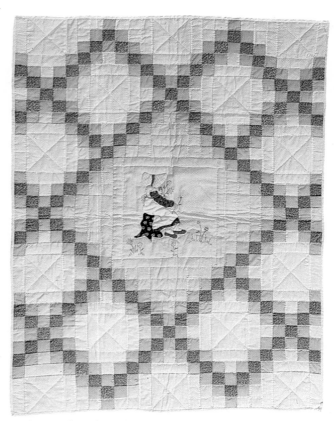

City Lady crib quilt: a Colonial Lady set in Double Irish Chain. Designed and made by the author in 1975. Author's collection.

Sunbonnet Sue quilt. Made in 1975 by Mabel Beaven for her granddaughter, Betsy Bergh.

Peeking Sue crib quilt. Designed and made by the author in 1977. Author's collection.

Sunbonnet Dolls, a king-sized quilt made for Anita Murphy by members of the Golden Triangle Quilt Guild of Beaumont, TX. Several blocks with pairs of Sunbonnets honor Mrs. Murphys's twin granddaughters. Collection of Anita Murphy.

Good Morning

Sunday

Seven Days of the Week I—c. 1905

This set was designed by Bernhardt Wall and was included in the 1910 *Ladies Art* needlework catalog. Originally the figures were meant for outline embroidery in either stem or split stitch, but I have drawn them to a larger size; you may either embroider or appliqué these figures to 12-inch square blocks.

Monday

Wednesday

Saturday

63

12-in. block

64

Idle Freddy and
Busy Sue—1920's

This delightful pair of Sunbonnets was taken from an old and treasured quilt pattern catalog printed in the 1920's, *Grandma Dexter's New Appliqué and Patchwork Designs*. The figures are examples of the rare short-pants, short-skirt variety. Two sizes are given for appliqué—one for a 10-inch and the other for a 12-inch square block. I have also included patterns for embroidery for 12-inch square blocks.

12-in. block

10-in. block

12-inch. block

68

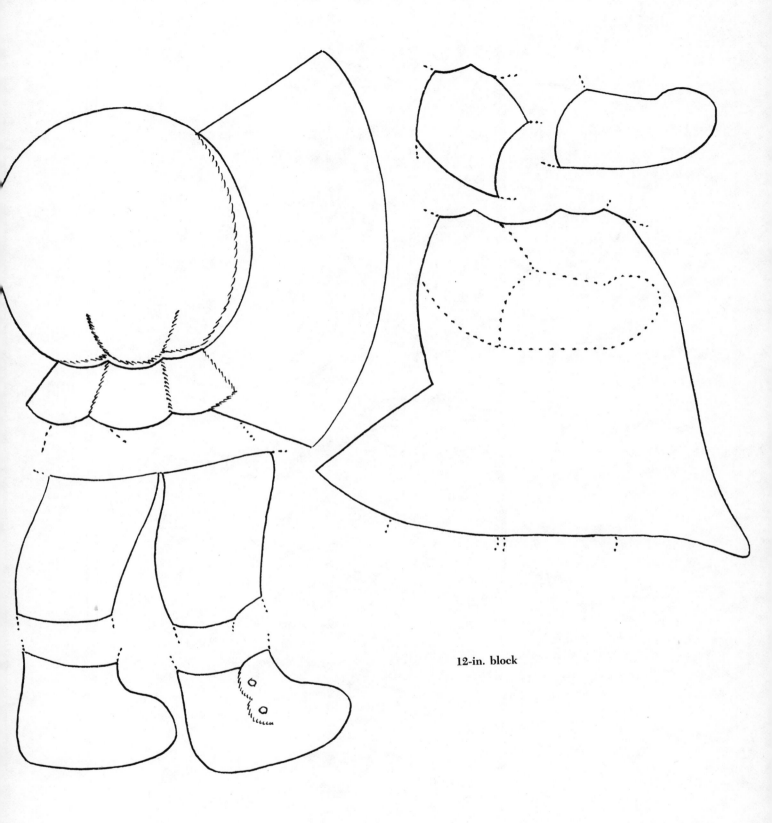

12-in. block

10-in. block

Sudden Sue (? date)

The name does not refer to the pose of this figure, but rather to the fact that the appliqué pattern has only one piece; it is finished with some simple daisy stitch and French knot embroidery. Using this pattern, your quilt top will be finished "Suddenly."

You may choose to cut out one figure and embroider directly on the appliqué piece, as shown in the first figure. Or you may prefer to cut out the figure and the background pieces for both the hatband and flowers, and embroider these. This block can be made in a different manner by using a print block and plain appliquéd figure. The patterns are drawn for both 10-inch and 12-inch square blocks.

10-in. block

71

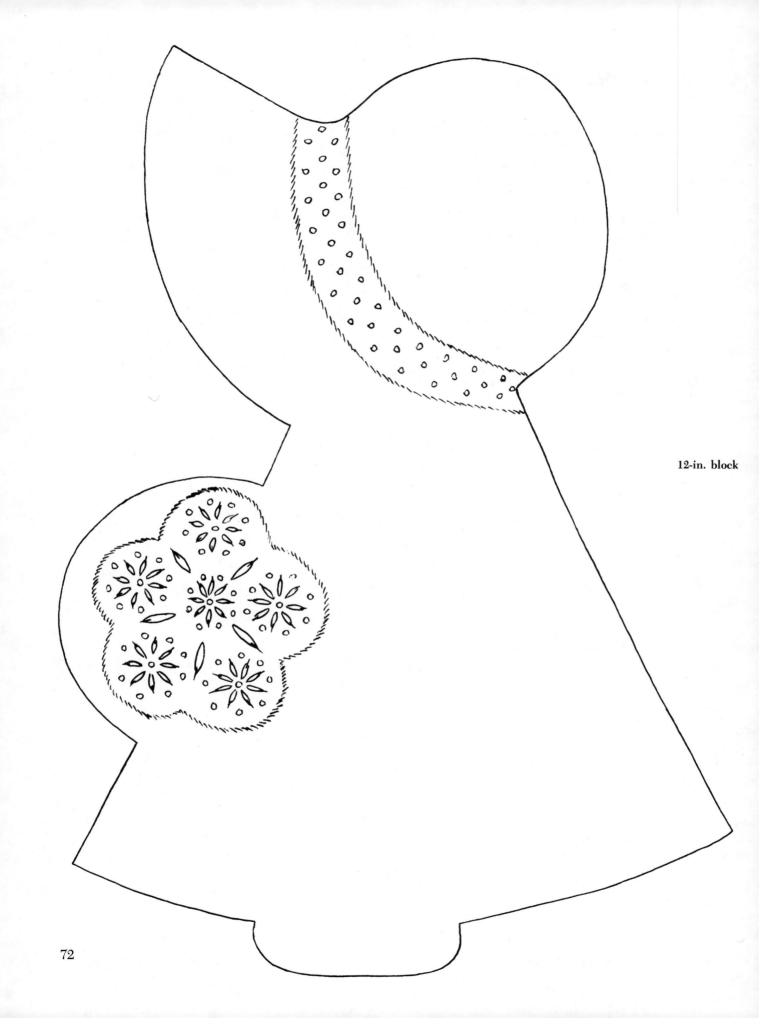

12-in. block

72

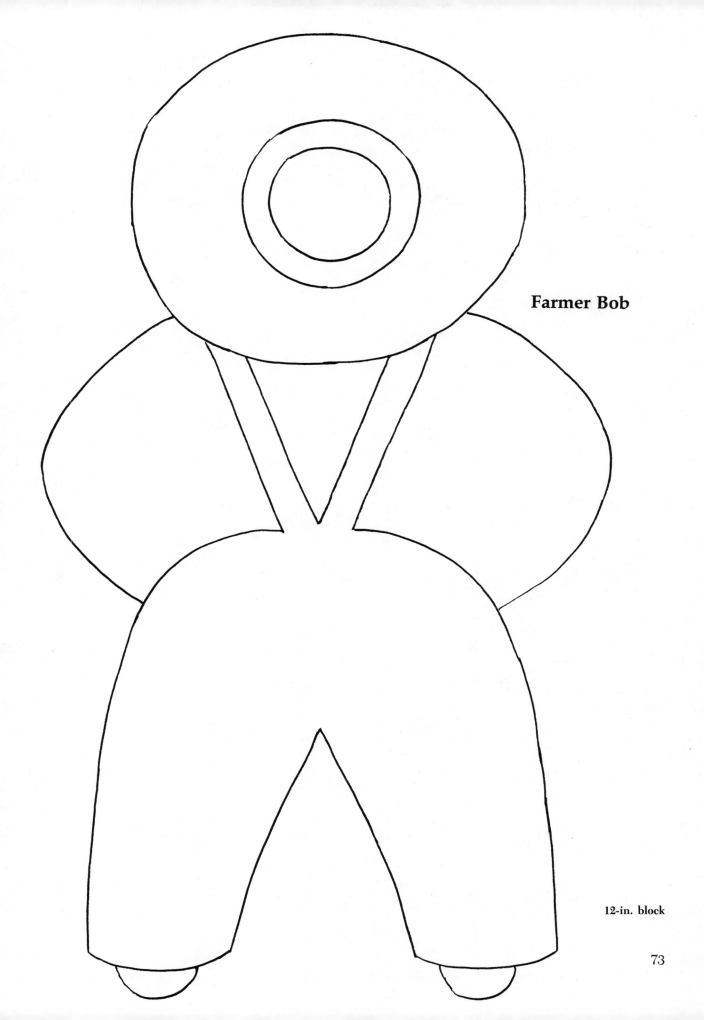

Farmer Bob

12-in. block

73

Farmer Bob—1920's

As traditional to Overall patterns as Traditional Sue is to Sunbonnet patterns, this design has been appliquéd on hundreds of quilts over the years. I have seen some blocks in this design with embroidered farming or gardening tools, sports accessories, etc., showing over the figure's shoulders. The hatband may be either embroidered or appliquéd.

The patterns are drawn for 12-inch square blocks in either embroidery or appliqué, or for 15-inch square blocks in appliqué.

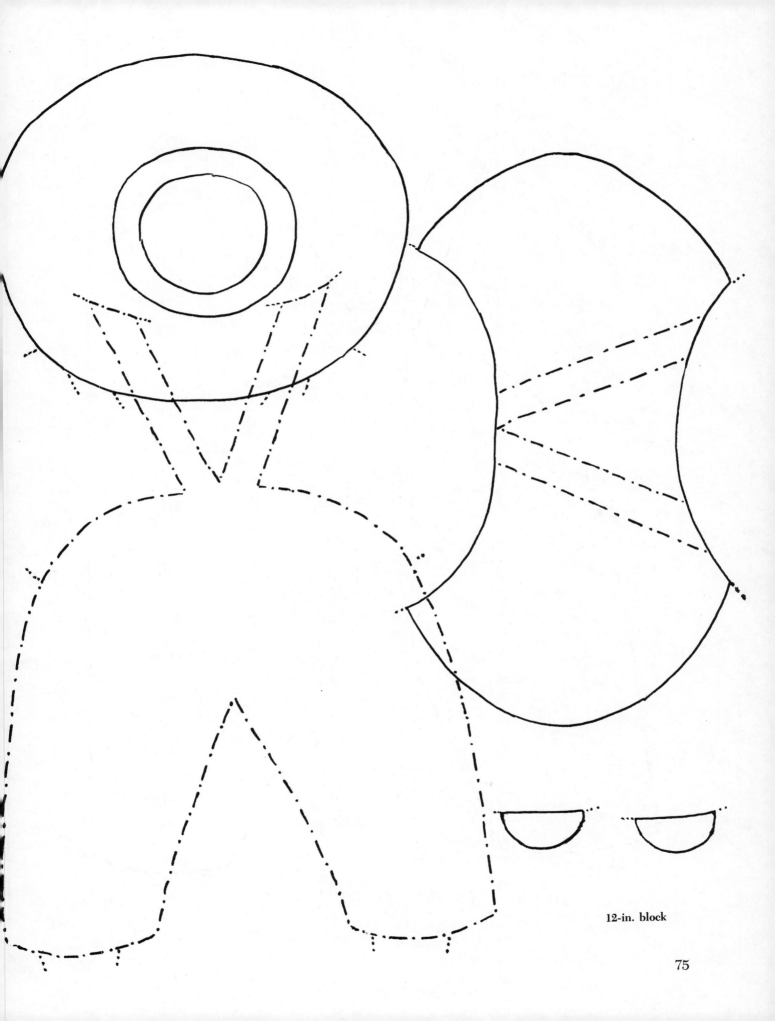

12-in. block

75

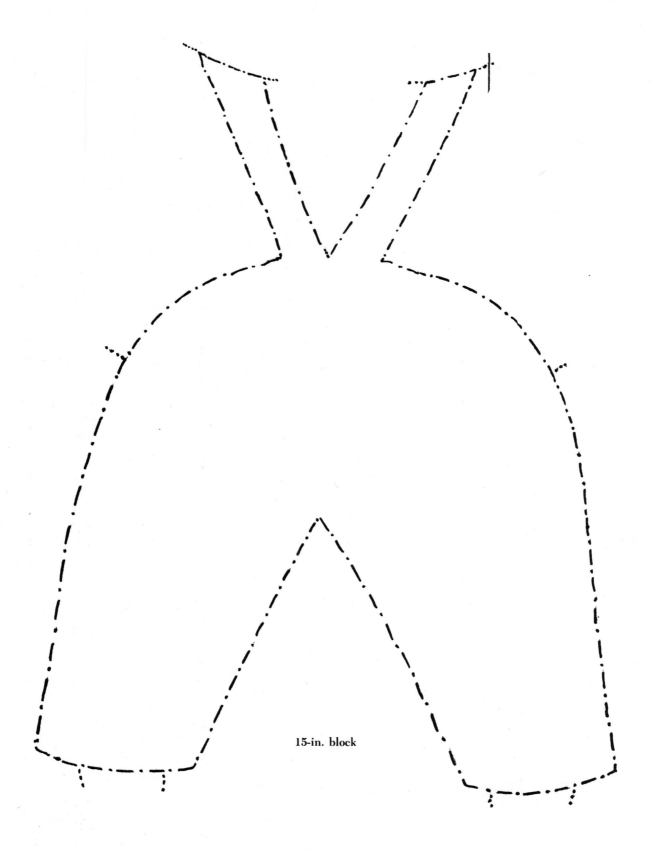

15-in. block

76

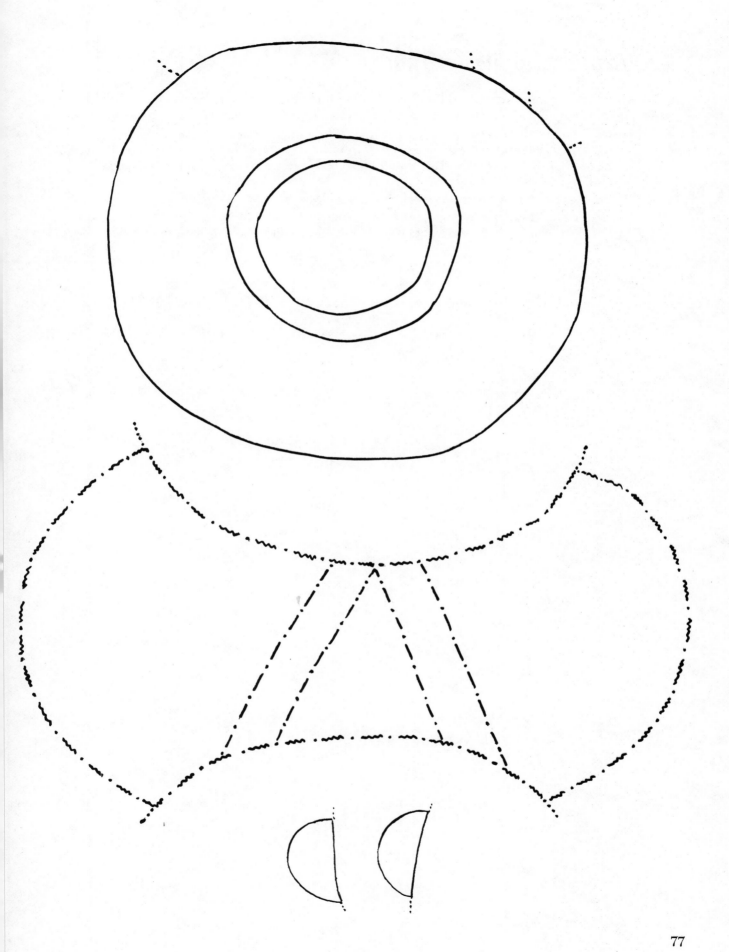

Traditional Sunbonnet Sue—1920's

I am including the simple, traditional Sunbonnet Sue because she is still loved by quilters in spite of having been around for so long. The patterns are drawn for a 12-inch square appliqué block.

Embroidery flower patterns are used in the pattern shown, but you may prefer to use a line of lace or rickrack trim. The dotted line of the thumb on the left hand should be embroidered.

Four examples of the traditional Sunbonnet Sue are shown in the Frontispiece. By moving the skirt hem backward or forward as shown, the stance can be changed so that the figure looks upward, down, or front. Extra accessories can be added with embroidery.

12-in. block

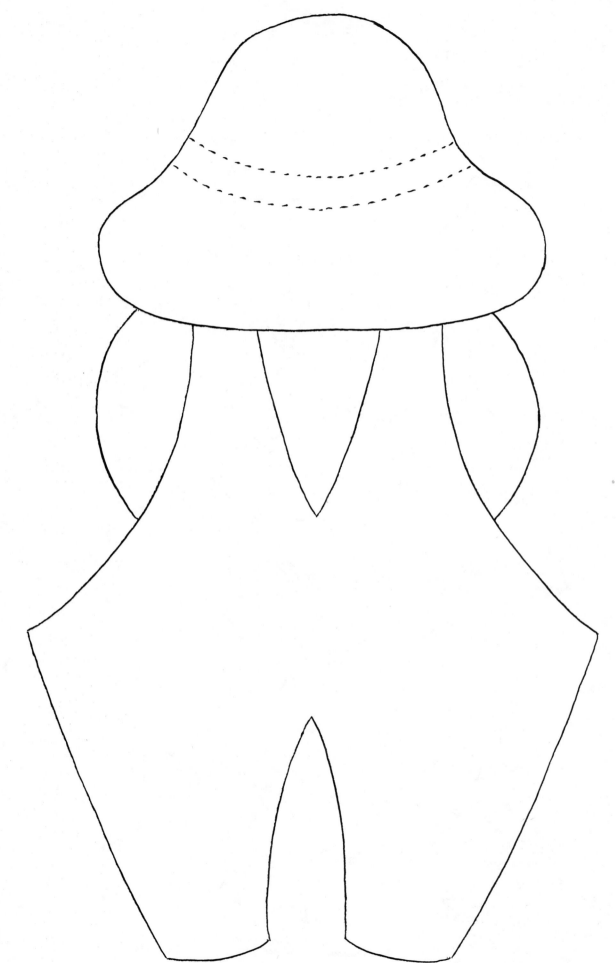

Overall Bill (? date)

This is a Tennessee pattern. Its special features are the side angles on the overalls, the hat, and the treatment (or non-treatment) of the feet.

The patterns are drawn for embroidery or appliqué in the 12-inch square size and for appliqué in the 15-inch square block size. Placed diagonally, the figures will also fit in 10- and 12-inch blocks.

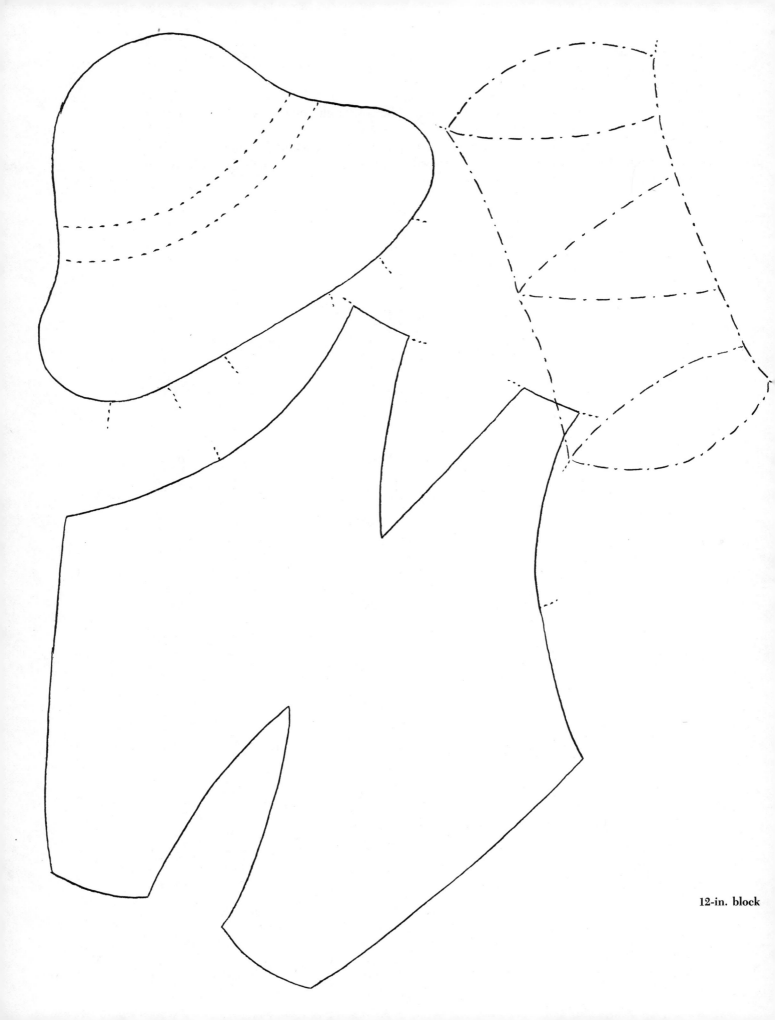

12-in. block

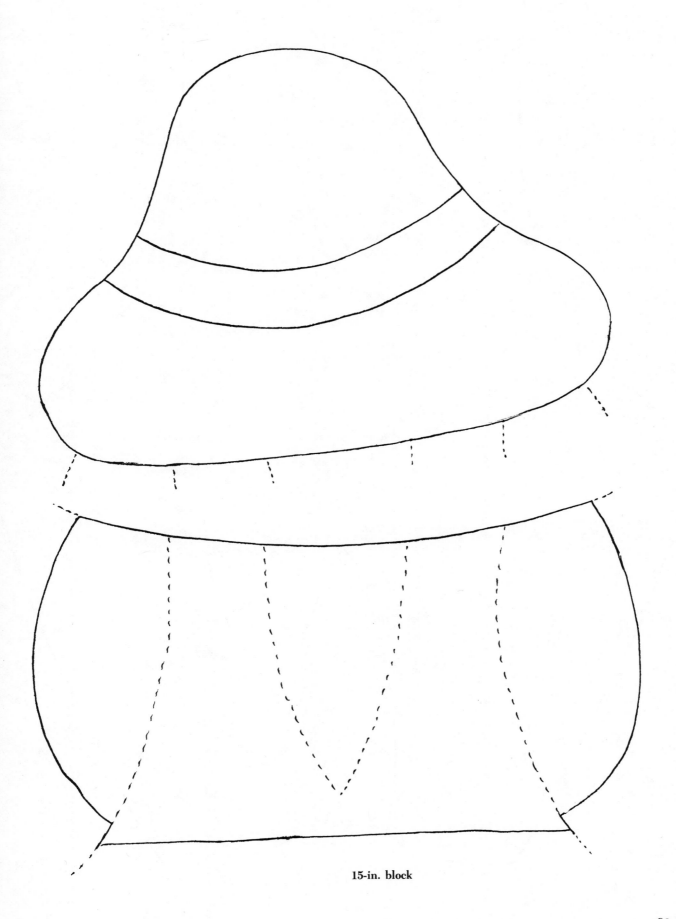

15-in. block

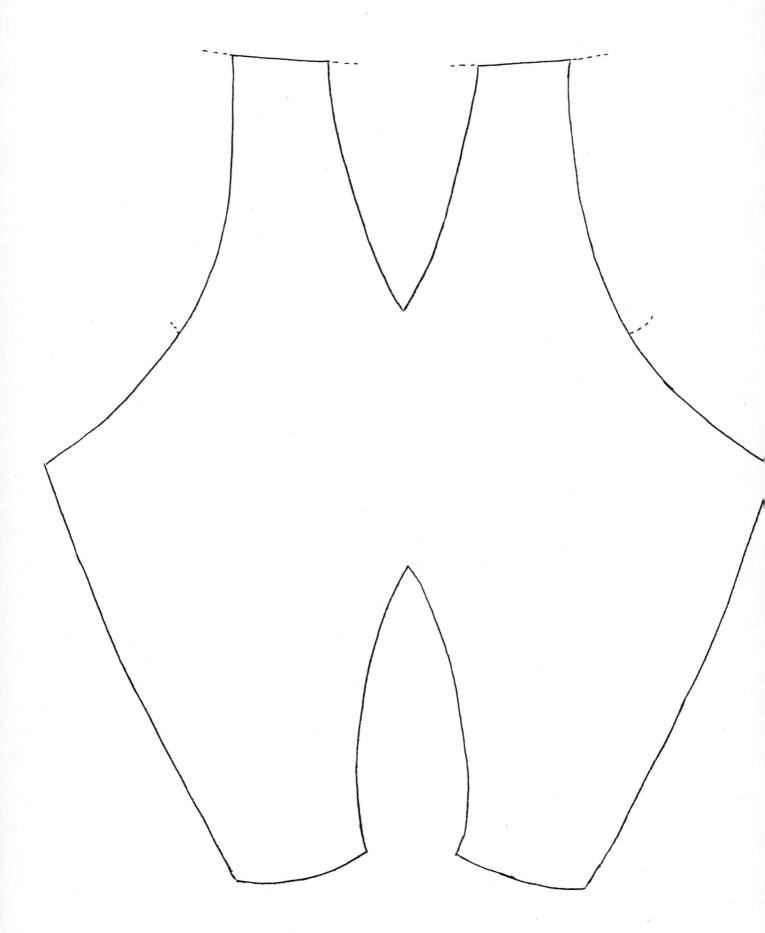

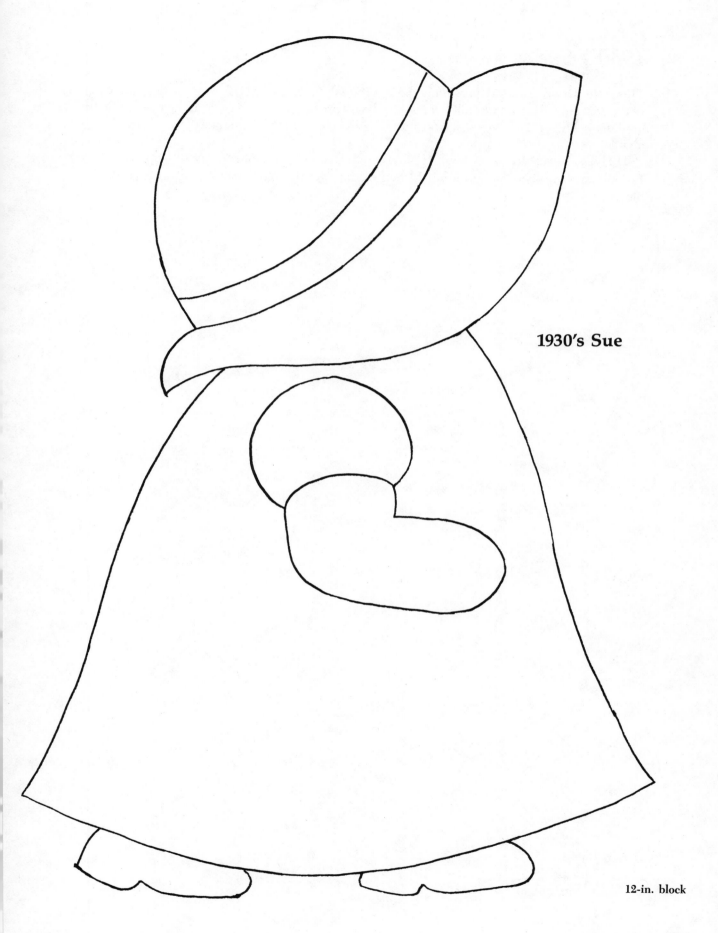

1930's Sue

12-in. block

1930's Sue

This is the Depression-era version of the traditional Sunbonnet. Her hat is an appliqué version of the summer straw/winter felt hat trimmed with grosgrain ribbon worn at the time by all little (and many bigger) girls. Also, she is quite chubby, showing the influence of the Grace Drayton characters.

The patterns are drawn for 12-inch squares in either embroidery or appliqué, or for 15-inch square blocks in appliqué. Placed diagonally, the figures fit on 10-inch and 12-in. blocks.

12-in. block

87

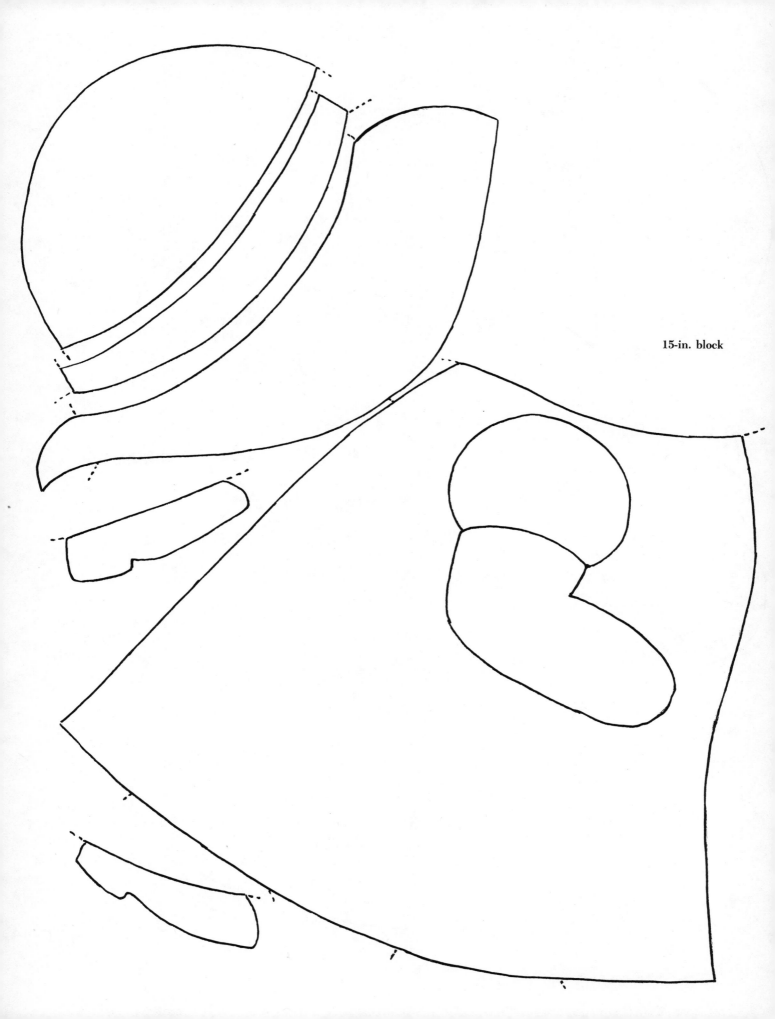

15-in. block

Peeking Sue

10-in. block

Peeking Sue and
Sunbonnet Sue II—1977

These two patterns are twins. One is as bashful as all other Sunbonnets, but the other just has to take a peek to see if anyone is noticing her. Their dress is a little fancier than is traditional; this enhances their effect when the figures are embroidered in the smaller size or appliquéd in the larger size.

The two patterns were each drawn in 10-inch square size for embroidery and appliqué and in 15-inch square block size for appliqué. Placed diagonally, the figures fit on 9-inch and 13-inch blocks.

10-in. block

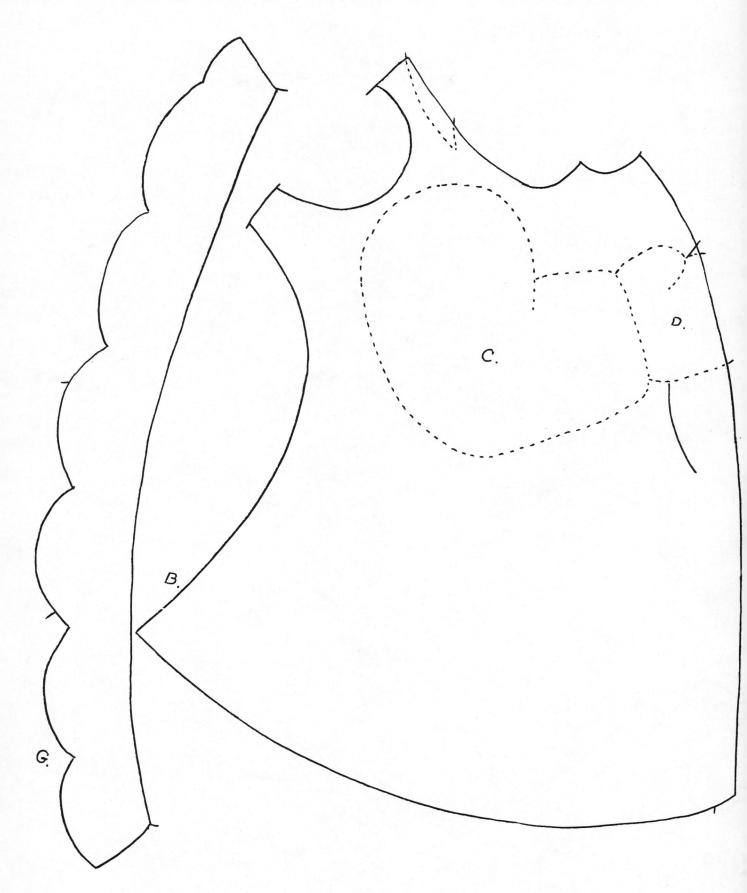

15-in. block

15-in. block

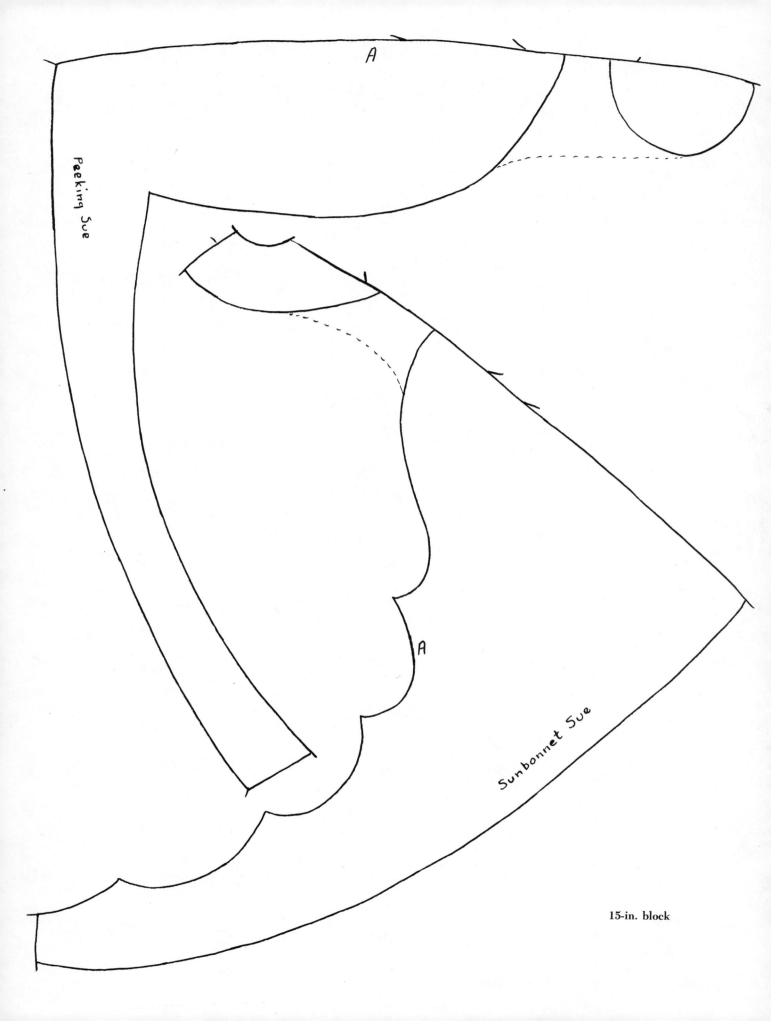

Peeking Sue

A

A

Sunbonnet Sue

15-in. block

10-in. block

95

96

10-in. block

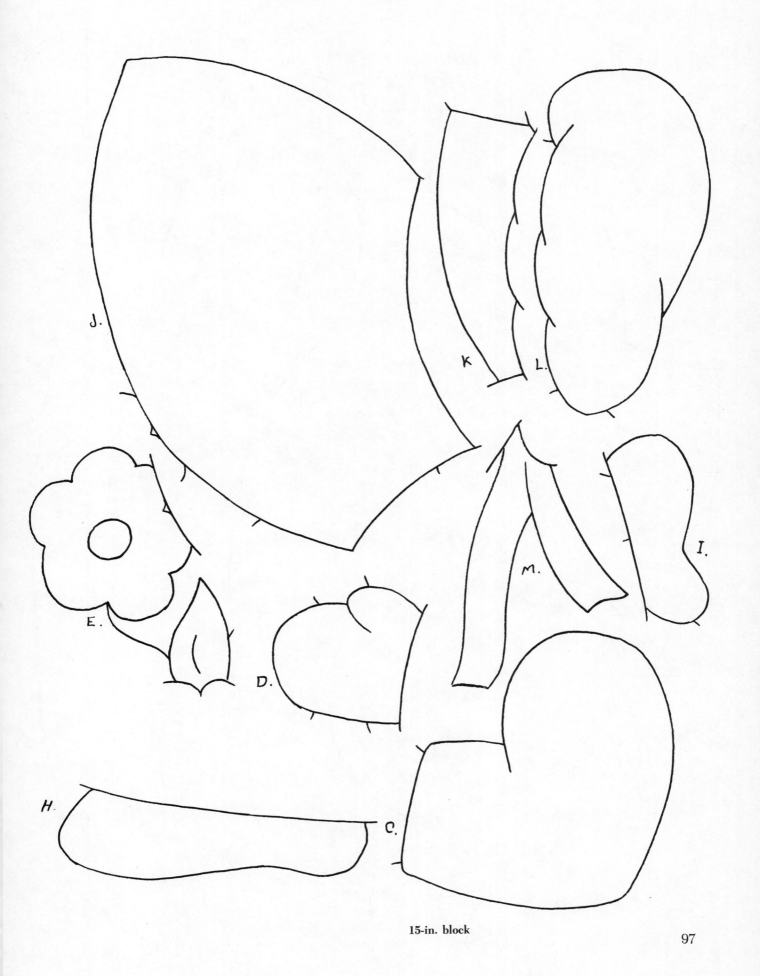

J.

K

L.

I.

E.

M.

D.

H.

C.

15-in. block

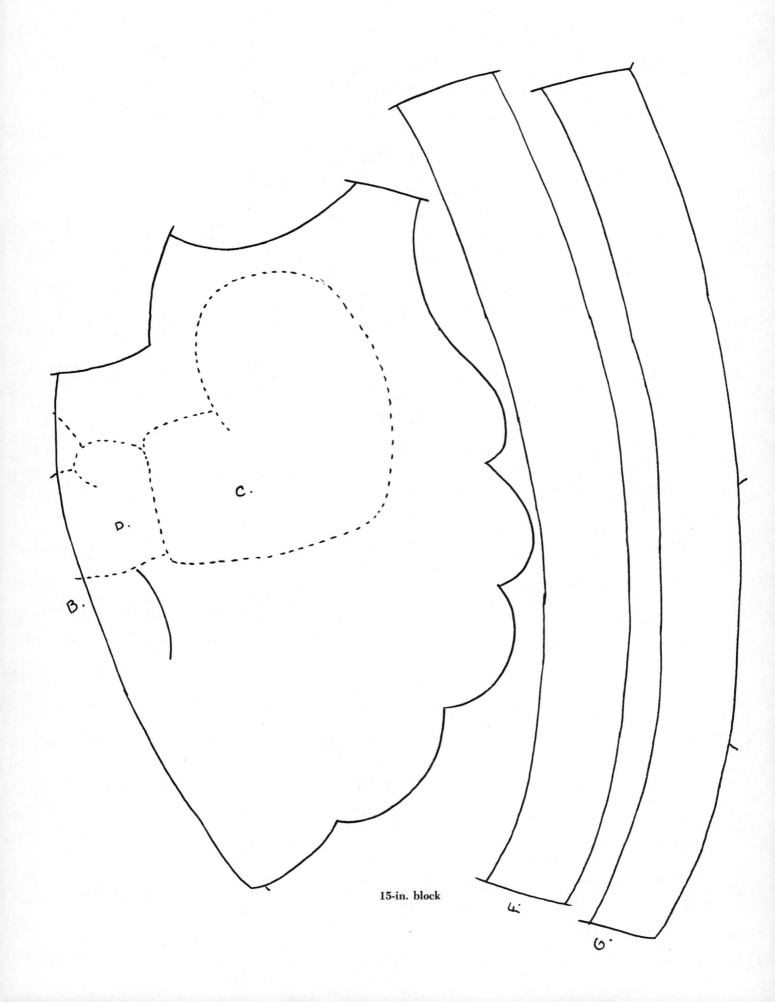

15-in. block

Springtime Mollie

12-in. block

Springtime Mollie—1935

Of all the Sunbonnets I have seen, this one may be the strangest in pattern. It incorporates many design fads of the Art Deco period—including the very fashionable (for little girls) black patent-leather "Mary Jane" shoes I was longing for myself at the time this design was published in *Woman's World* magazine.

The patterns are designed for a 6-inch square in embroidery, 12-inch squares in either embroidery or appliqué, and 18-inch squares in appliqué. The slanted-dash lines on the bonnet, plant, shoes, and pantalettes should be embroidered; the dots on the pantalettes should be French knots. The sash bow may also be embroidered if you wish.

6-in. block

12-in. block

18-in. block

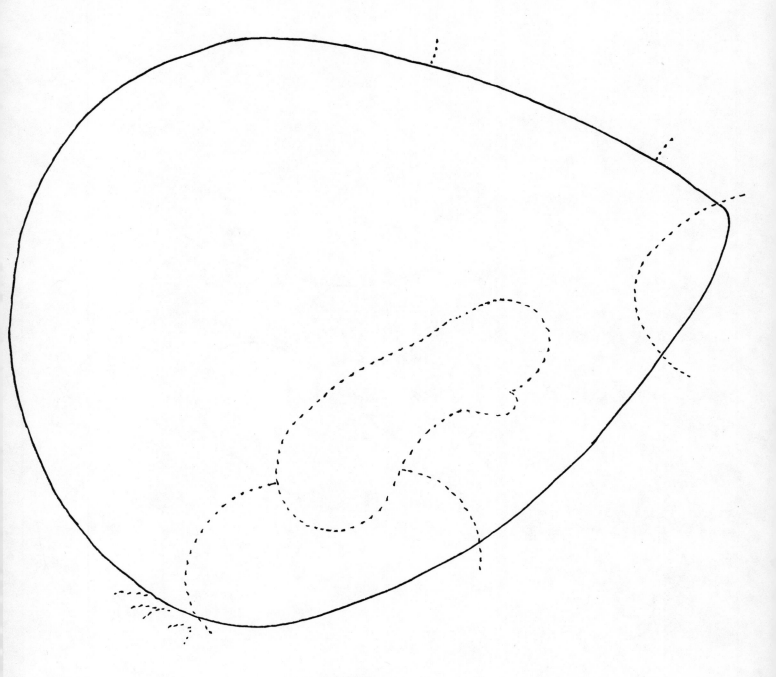

18-in. block

103

Merry March—1935

Although this is a more traditional design, I can see some design affiliation between it and both Springtime Mollie and Sudden Sue. I wonder if they were all designed by the same artist. This design was found in the Hall-Kretsinger book *The Romance of the Patchwork Quilt in America* (Plate LV, p. 190). It was named Sunbonnet Baby by the quilt's maker, Mrs. H.S. Stevenson; however, I did not consider the name entirely appropriate, so I've changed it for this book's design, the earliest I have been able to find of the kind of Sunbonnet I have termed the "wind-blown" type.

Her flowers, curls, shoes, and eyelet should all be embroidered. The pattern is drawn for a 12-inch square block in either embroidery or appliqué.

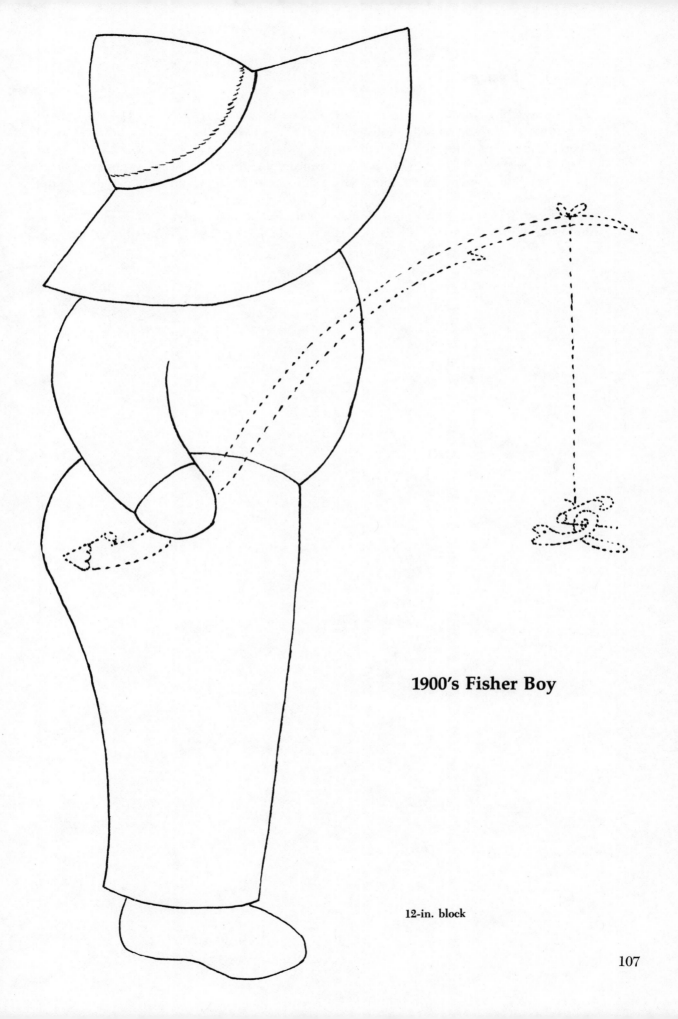

1900's Fisher Boy

12-in. block

107

1900's Fisher Boy

The earliest boy companions to the Sunbonnets did not wear overalls. As babies they are shown wearing apron smocks similar to the girls', as is the Buster Brown boy on page 131. When depicted as older, the boy figures wear a shirt and pants, as does this one. His manly, chest-out pose is very typical of turn-of-the-century illustrations. It was this pose that inspired me to give him a popgun in addition to his fishing pole. A flag would work very well with this pattern, too.

The patterns are drawn for a 10-inch square in appliqué and a 12-inch square in either embroidery or appliqué. The accessories and hatband may be either appliquéd or embroidered, as you wish.

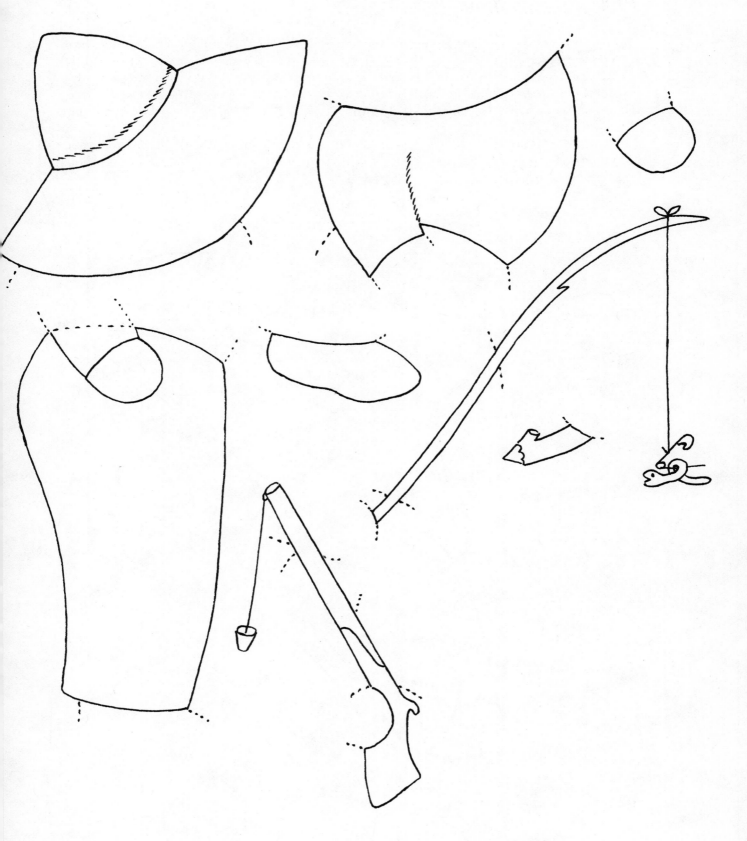

10-in. block

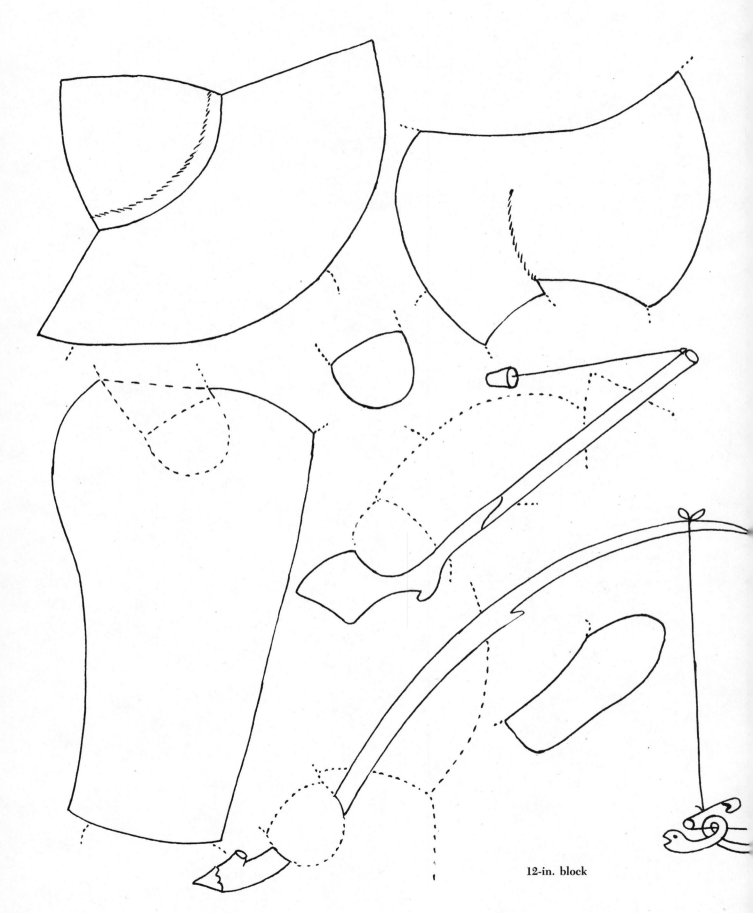

12-in. block

Sunbonnet Girl

12-in. block

111

Sunbonnet Girl and
Overall Boy—1920's

A 1920's quilt pattern pamphlet of twelve pages is the origin of this Sunbonnet pair. The girl is one of the rare short-skirted figures, while the boy wears the usual overalls in a slightly different form.

The pair's hatbands are both embroidered, as are the girl's shoes and the boy's overall straps and buttons. The patterns are drawn for 10-inch squares in appliqué and 12-inch squares in both appliqué and embroidery.

this

'B'   'A'   'C'

12-in. block

113

'B' 'A' 'C'

10-in. block

114

12-in. block

115

Chase

10-in. block

116

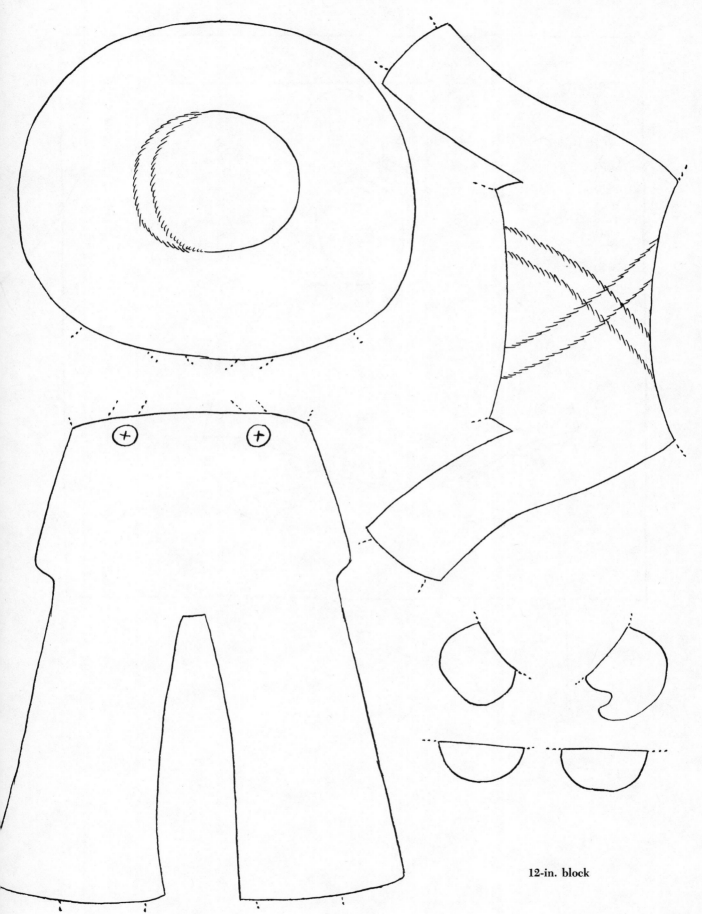

12-in. block

117

Seven Days of the Week II—1947

For a few years following the second World War, packets of embroidery pattern sets were available in the needlework departments of local dime stores. This group of designs were meant to be embroidered on dish-towel sets—one towel for each day in a week. My friends and I embroidered many sets of these towels for our homes. Unfortunately, I did not find this set of designs at that time; the patterns here are from a friend's collection. The inscription not only tells the day of the week (as was usual) but gives the activity assigned to that day by the traditional housewives' rhyme.

These patterns are drawn only for the 6-inch squares of the original patterns.

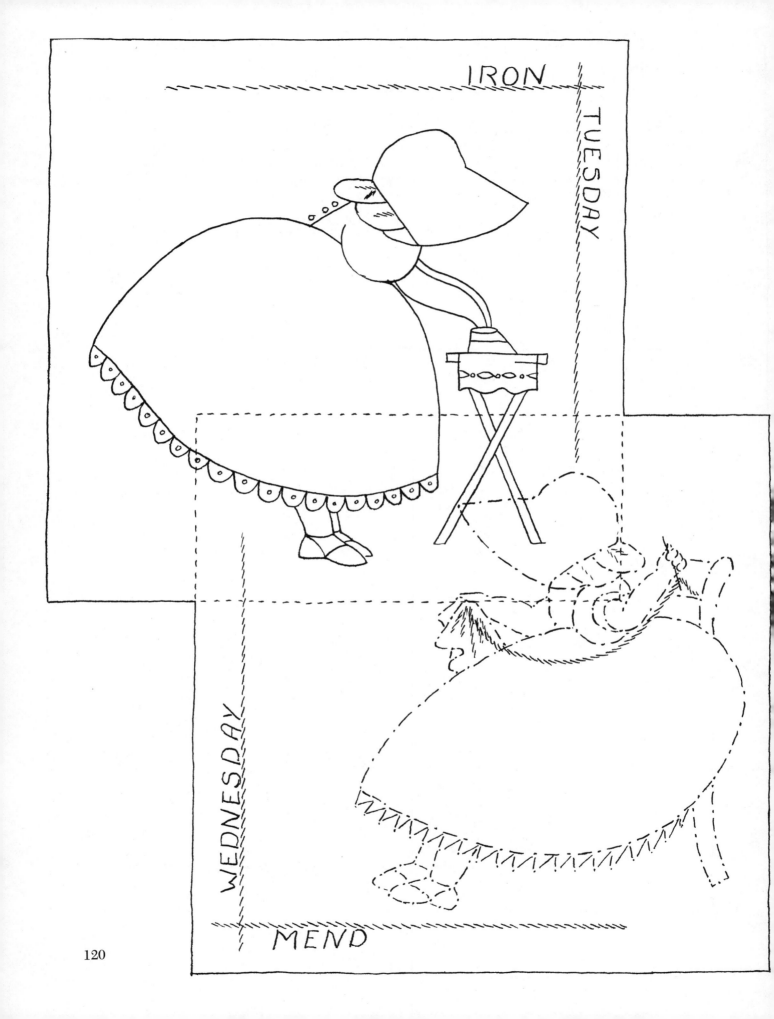

IRON

TUESDAY

WEDNESDAY

MEND

120

6-in. block

Little Sunbonnet

10-in. block

Little Sunbonnet and
Little Fisherman—1960's

There are several very simple pattern designs among the Sunbonnets, but none simpler than these two. The girl is just two appliqué pieces and embroidery trim; the boy is three appliqué pieces and embroidery. They were not added to my collection as a set but arrived individually. The girl was given to me by a friend (and several years later I again saw the pattern in a magazine). The boy came straight from a baby quilt made by an elderly lady who has used this design for several years. If the figures were not designed by the same person, they were still designed with the same economy of line and make a fine set.

The patterns are drawn for either embroidery or appliqué in the sizes for 6-inch, 10-inch, and 12-inch square blocks.

12-in. block

125

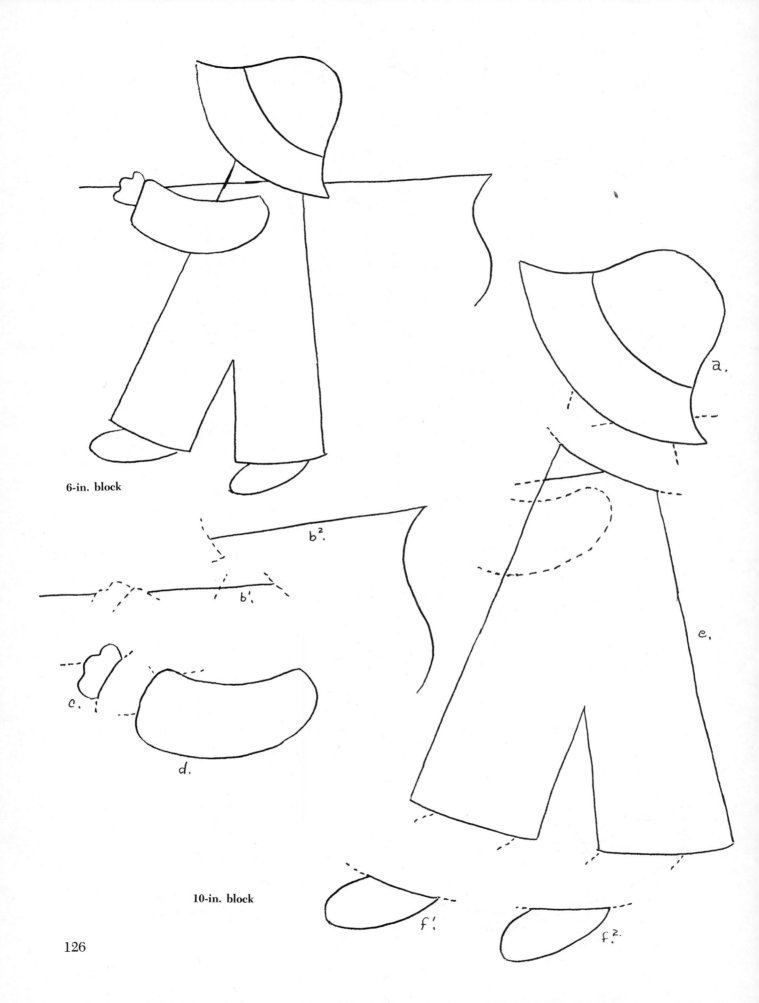

6-in. block

10-in. block

126

1.

2.

12-in. block

127

128

Lazy Mobcap (right) *and*
Lazy Mobcap (left)—1922

These cute Sunbonnet types lounging in their armchairs were published in the Needlework Department of *Woman's World* magazine under the by-line of John Then (see page 13). They were shown on the apron of the figure copied as an illustration in this book (see page 16, 1a). I've added the book and footstool to the figure facing left.

The patterns were drawn for 12-inch squares in embroidery, but they can easily be separated for appliqué if you prefer that method.

Buster Brown Boy

Buster Brown Boy—1912

This figure is a boy, not originally drawn as a pattern but part of an illustration for clothing in *The Home Instructor* magazine. I did not have to adapt it at all. It was in illustrations such as this and not only from the designs in the needlework columns that many quilters found the inspiration for their patterns. The boy wears the coverall apron of a very small child's play outfit.

The pattern has been drawn for 12-inch square blocks in either embroidery or appliqué.

Little Lacy—1928

An interesting Sunbonnet variation from *Needlecraft, The Home Arts Magazine*, this figure is almost—but not quite—a Colonial Lady. The name Lacy (not Lucy) is an old Southern name, and it seems to suit her. In the original design the skirt was cut from a fancy eyelet material, the blouse from a plain pink, and the bonnet from a plain yellow material. The remainder of the figure was outline embroidery and French knots. I have never found a daintier Sunbonnet design.

The patterns are drawn for a 12-inch square in either all embroidery or all appliqué. You may use the original method of half-appliqué, half-embroidery if you prefer. The dotted lines indicate embroidery necessary to the all-appliqué design.

Sunbonnet Susy

8-in. block

137

Sunbonnet Susy—1916

The origin of this pattern was a browned newspaper clipping sent to me from a friend's collection just for this manuscript. The date was included but not the newspaper's name. The clipping showed an illustration of a series of patterns for Sunbonnets on the farm, and was intended for the use of 4-H Club girls. The designs were quite crude, but I enjoyed this one and thought you might like it also. This Sunbonnet is quite matronly, unlike most of the other patterns.

The patterns have been drawn for an 8-inch square block in embroidery or for a 12-inch square block in appliqué with embroidery touches. The dotted lines indicate placement of the moon (A) and the cat (B).

A

B

12-in. block

139

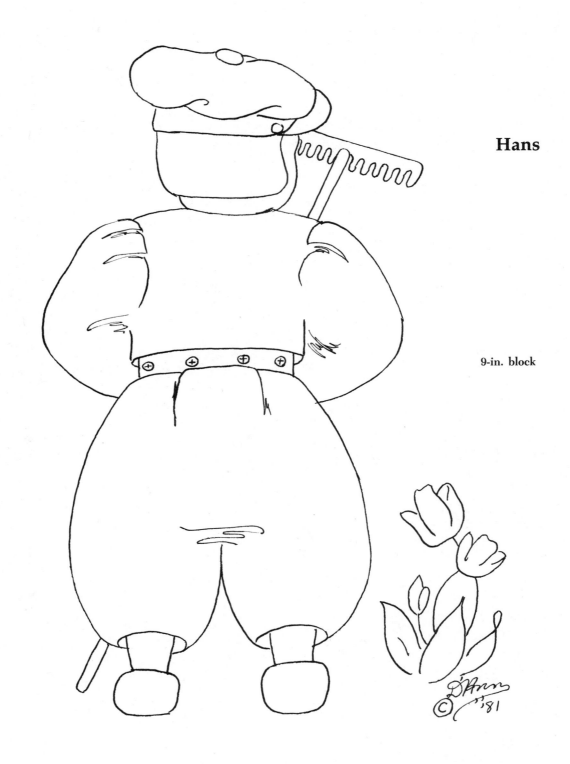

Hans

9-in. block

Dutch Dolls and Colonial Ladies

140

Three Dutch Dolls:
Hans—(1981), Tre'na, and
Katinka—(1920's)

The two girls are from an undated 1920's quilt pattern leaflet of twelve pages. The boy was added to make a set. Because the traditional Dutchman's costume is bulky, the boy does not look quite in scale with the girls, but he is.

The patterns are drawn for 9-inch squares for embroidery and 12-inch squares in either embroidery or appliqué. These patterns translate well to other media, such as leaded glass.

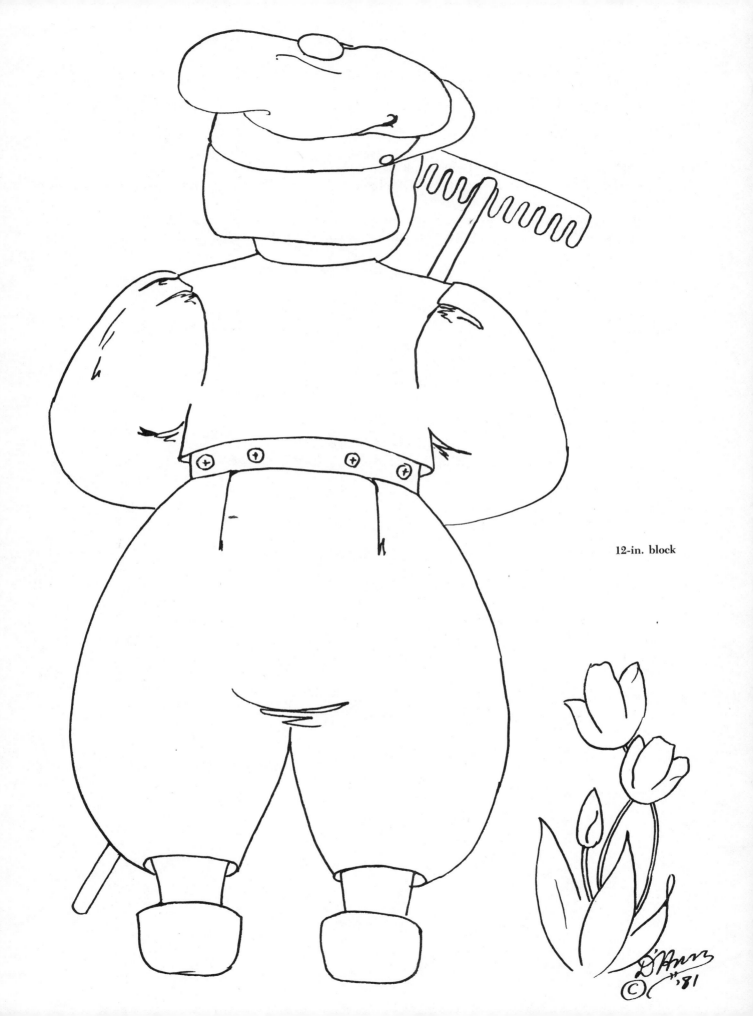

12-in. block

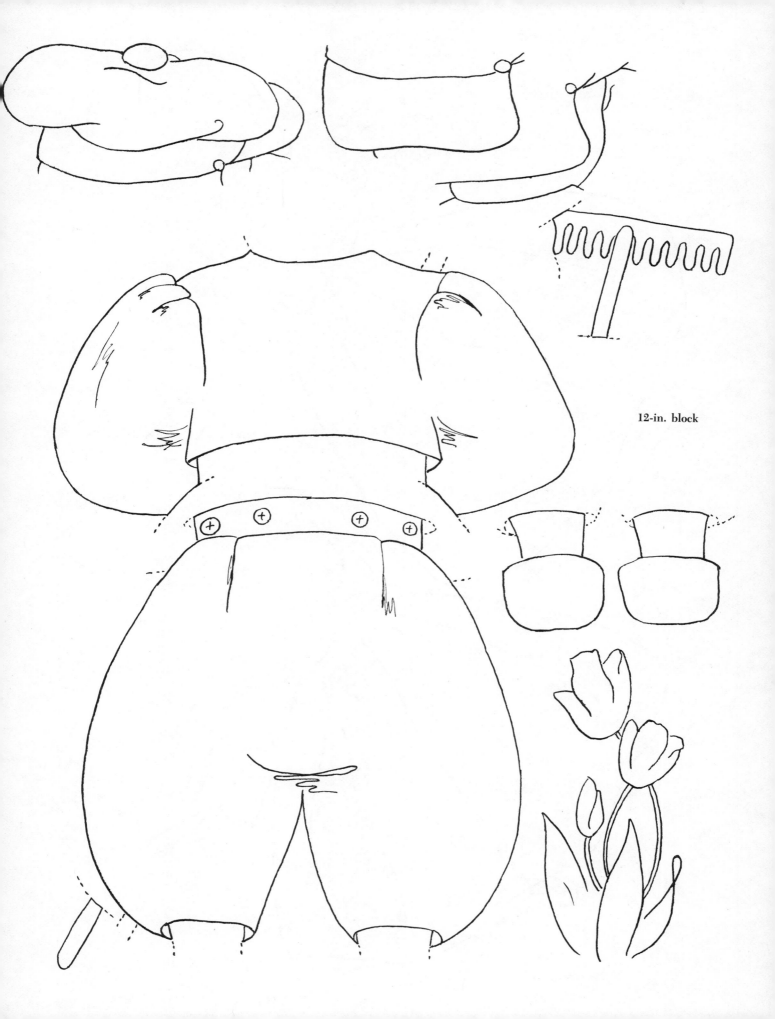

12-in. block

Tre′na

9-in. blocks
Katinka

144

12-in. block

145

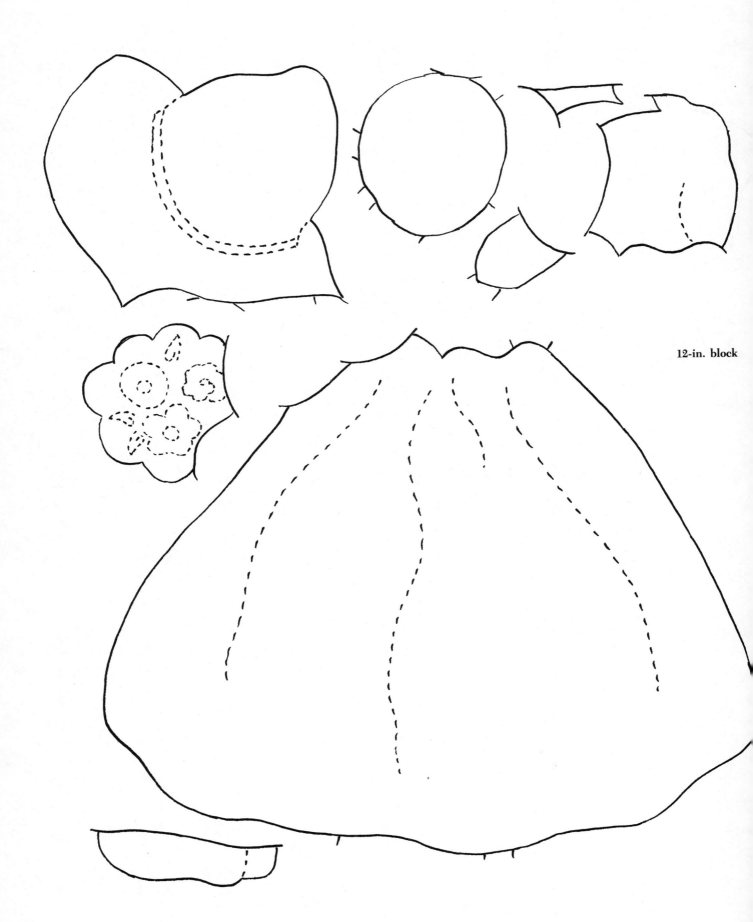

12-in. block

12-in. block

12-in. block

Dutch Doll (side)

149

Dutch Doll (side) and
Dutch Doll (back)—1933

Ruby Short McKim designed this Dutch Doll set. It was published in *Woman's World* magazine a little later than Betty Blue (page 47). The hat on these figures seems to be an imaginative cross between a Dutch bonnet and a mobcap. I do like the inclusion of each figure's own pet cat, as I think cats and needlework go together. (I have received many photos of quilts that also include the owner's cat, so I am not alone in my opinion.)

The patterns are drawn for 12-inch squares in either embroidery or appliqué. The dotted lines show where the cats should sit.

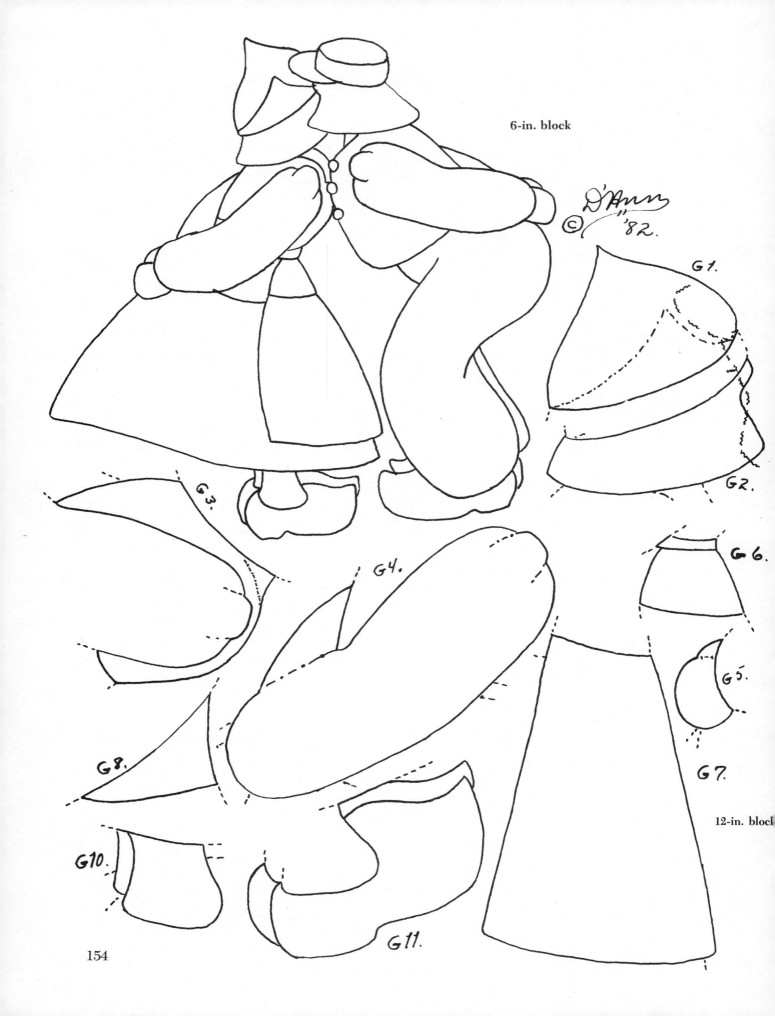

6-in. block

G1.

G2.

G3.

G4.

G6.

G5.

G7.

G8.

12-in. block

G10.

G11.

154

Kissing Dutch Dolls—1982

Tiptoeing through the tulips leads to complications, and this is just one of them. Wouldn't this be a cute pattern for a newlyweds' quilt? The figures can be used both singly and together on the blocks. They might also be placed with their backs together to symbolize that first quarrel.

The patterns have been drawn for a 6-inch square block in embroidery (and can also be used on matching pillow cases), and for a 12-inch square block in appliqué for a quilt. The squiggled dash lines on the girl's hat and hair indicate the overlap of the boy's figure when they kiss. The pieces for the girl's figure are marked g, and the boy's b.

B1.

B4.

B2.

B3.

B5.

B7.

B6.

G9.

12-in. block

Mandarin Girl and
Mandarin Boy—1982

When compiling the patterns for this manuscript I tried to think of other cultures in which a sunbonnet or its equivalent is a traditional part of the native costume. The only one I could think of immediately was the straw hat of the Chinese. So here is a pair of "Chinese Dutch" Dolls to give your quilts an international flavor.

The patterns are drawn for 6-inch square blocks in embroidery and 12-inch squares in appliqué.

6-in. block

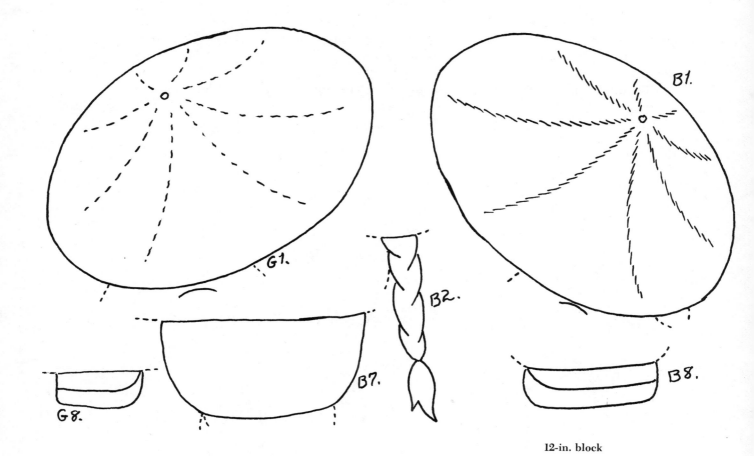

G1.

B1.

B2.

G8.

B7.

B8.

12-in. block

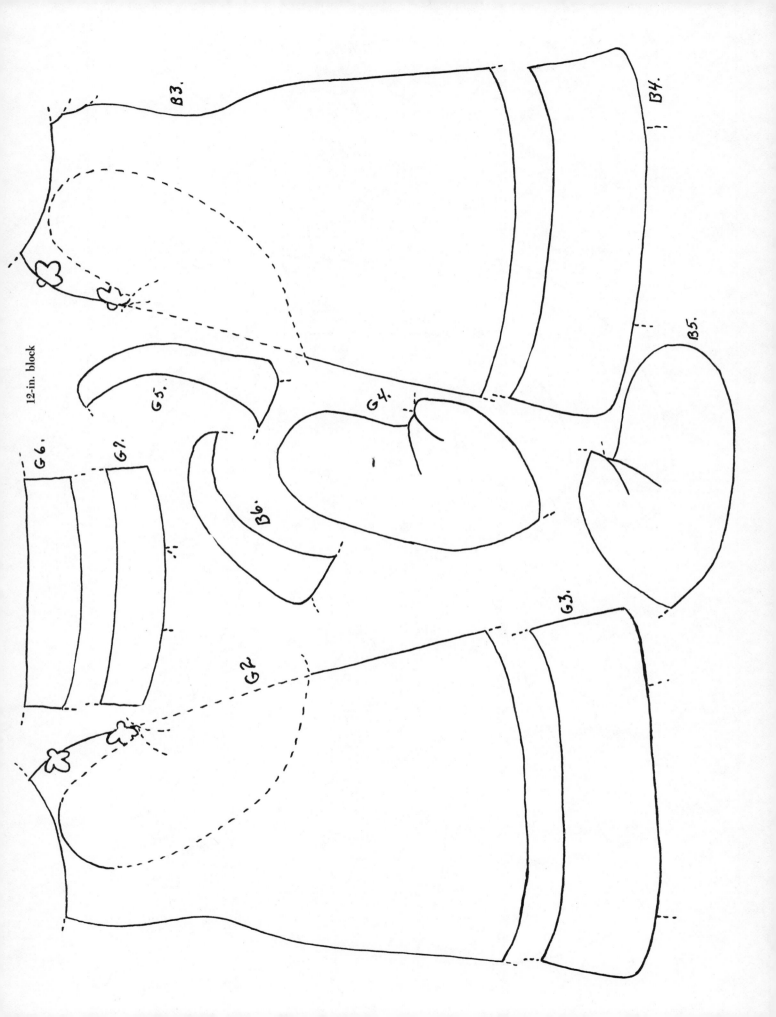

B3.

B4.

B5.

12-in. block

G5.

G4.

G6.

G7.

B6.

G2

G3.

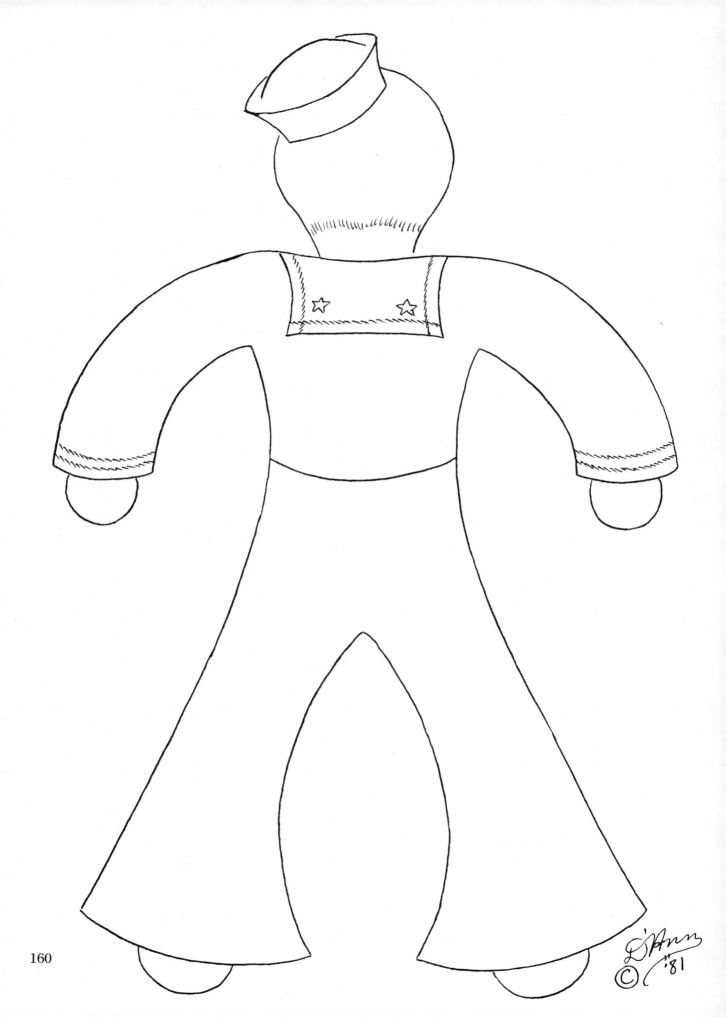

160

Sailor Simon—1942

It took some thought before I decided to place this sailor among the Dutch Dolls. Then I thought of the old recruiting slogan, "Join the Navy and see the world."

I don't remember when I first designed this swaggering Tar, but it must have been while I was in school and the War was not very old. Since I designed him before I started collecting quilt patterns in earnest, the date given with my signature is when I drew him as a pattern.

The uniform of the U.S. sailors was altered several years ago, eliminating the bell-bottom trousers and sailor collar. However, in the last couple of years the uniform has been returned to the traditional style because of requests from the sailors themselves.

This pattern has been drawn for 12-inch square blocks in either appliqué or embroidery.

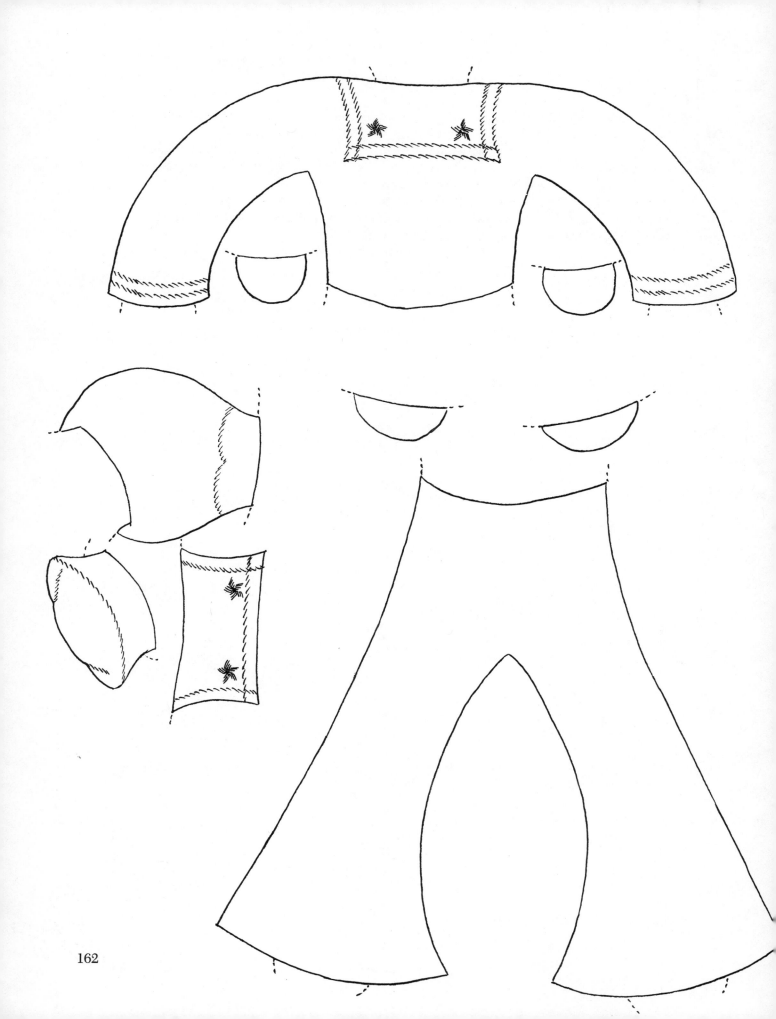

162

Little Sailor

Little Sailor—1909

This is another little figure from *The Home Instructor's Magazine* (as was the Buster Brown Boy), only this boy was part of a cover illustration.

The patterns were drawn for 12-inch squares in either embroidery or appliqué. The details and background should be embroidered whichever method you choose.

165

166

12-in. block

Colonial Flower Girl and
Colonial Garden Girl—1921

This is another set from the prolific designers in the Needlework Department of *Woman's World* magazine. It was suggested in the magazine column that they be used on pillow covers, but they are perfect for quilt blocks as well.

The patterns have been drawn for either embroidery or appliqué in the 12-inch square size and for appliqué with embroidered trim in the 18-inch square size. This last can be used for the center of baby quilts or for a medallion quilt. It can also be used as the center block of top design Nos. 5, 6, 7, or 8, page 19.

12-in. block

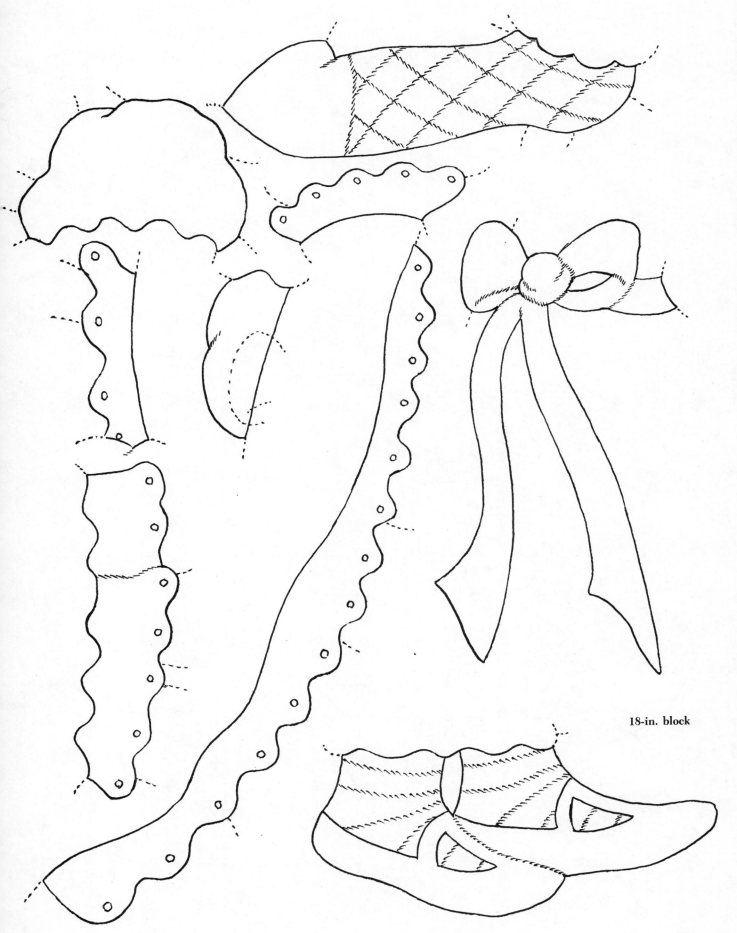

18-in. block

169

18-in. block

170

Colonial Garden Girl

12-in. block

a | a

12-in. block

18-in. block

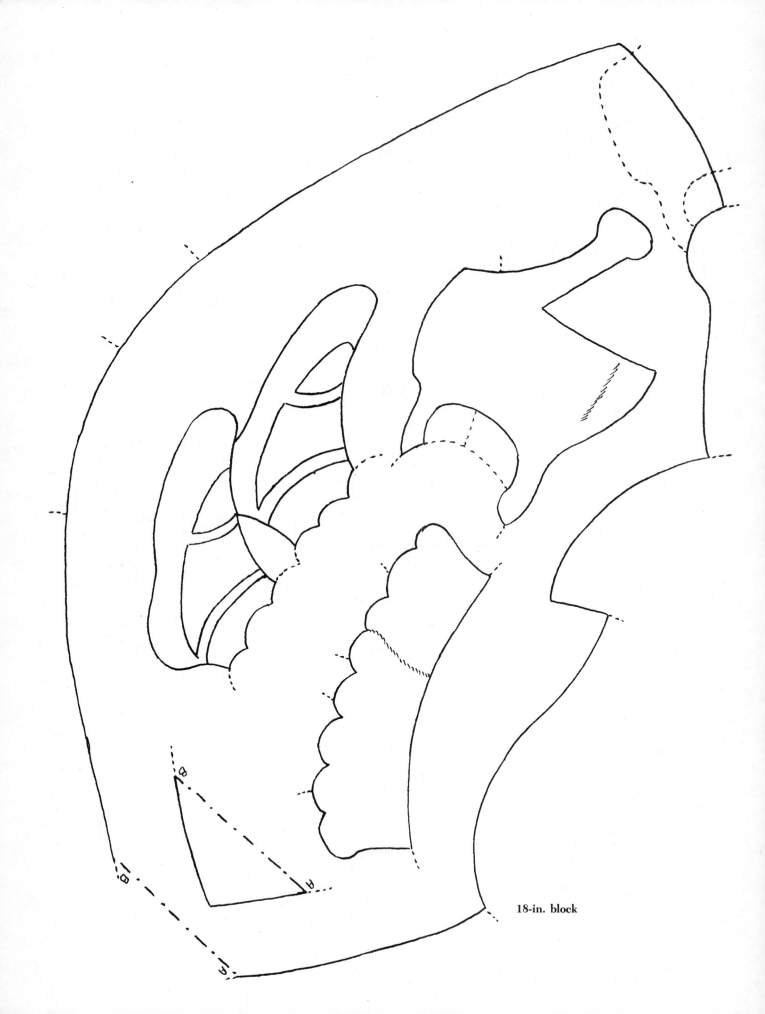

18-in. block

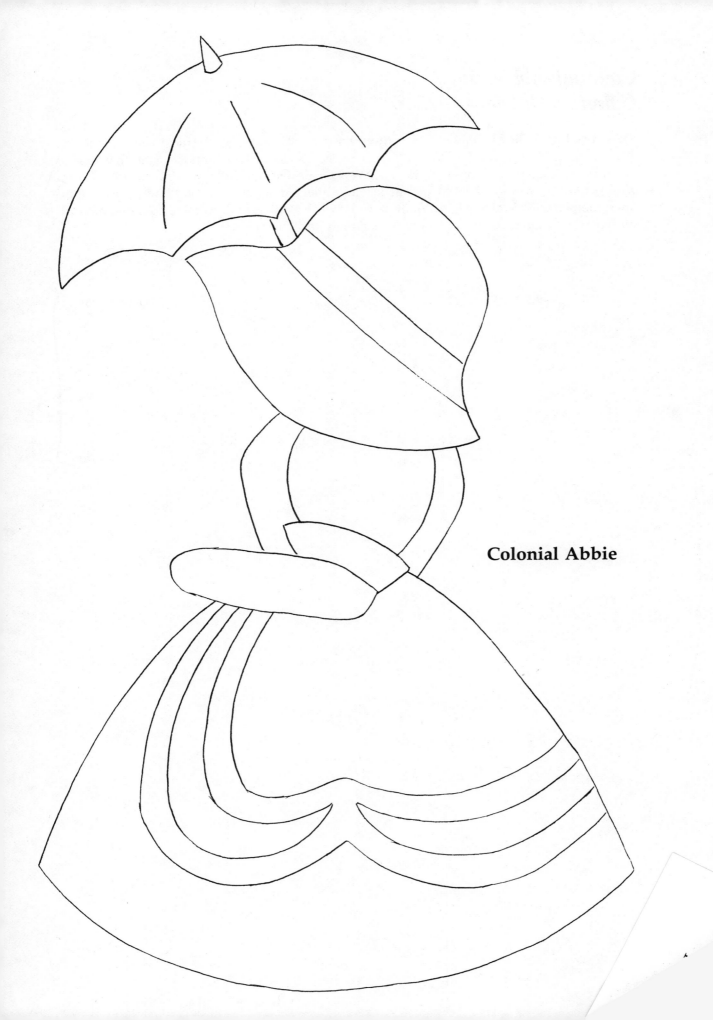

Colonial Abbie

Colonial Abbie and
Colonial Hattie—1925

These two little ladies are copies from a quilt shown in Plate LIII of the Hall-Kretsinger book, *The Romance of the Patchwork Quilt in America* (p. 188). The caption states that it is a "Child's quilt, adapted from a (Marie D.) Webster design by Carrie A. Hall, in 1925." The patterns are drawn for 12-inch squares in embroidery, but they can be divided easily into appliqué patterns. In the original quilt, each lady has a different decorative appliqué pattern on her skirt. I have given the two most elaborate designs.

Colonial Hattie

Selling Flowers—1933

This street vendor was first published in the same magazine column that gave us the designs for Colonial Flower Girl and Colonial Garden Girl—the Needlework Department of *Woman's World.*

    The pattern was drawn for a 12-inch square block in appliqué, but it can be divided into an appliqué-and-embroidery pattern easily.

12-in. block

180

Spring Showers—1979

A few years ago, I wrote and illustrated a magazine series about the history of American quilting. For one of the illustrations, a 1930's bedroom, I could not find a suitable quilt-top design among the patterns in my collection. So I just drew in a design that fit. Afterward, I decided it was a good design to include in this manuscript, and I drew these patterns. I hope you like this lady, too.

The patterns are drawn for a 12-inch square in either embroidery or appliqué with embroidery, and for an 18"-by-22" oblong quilt center in appliqué with embroidery.

12-in. block

18-in. × 22-in. block

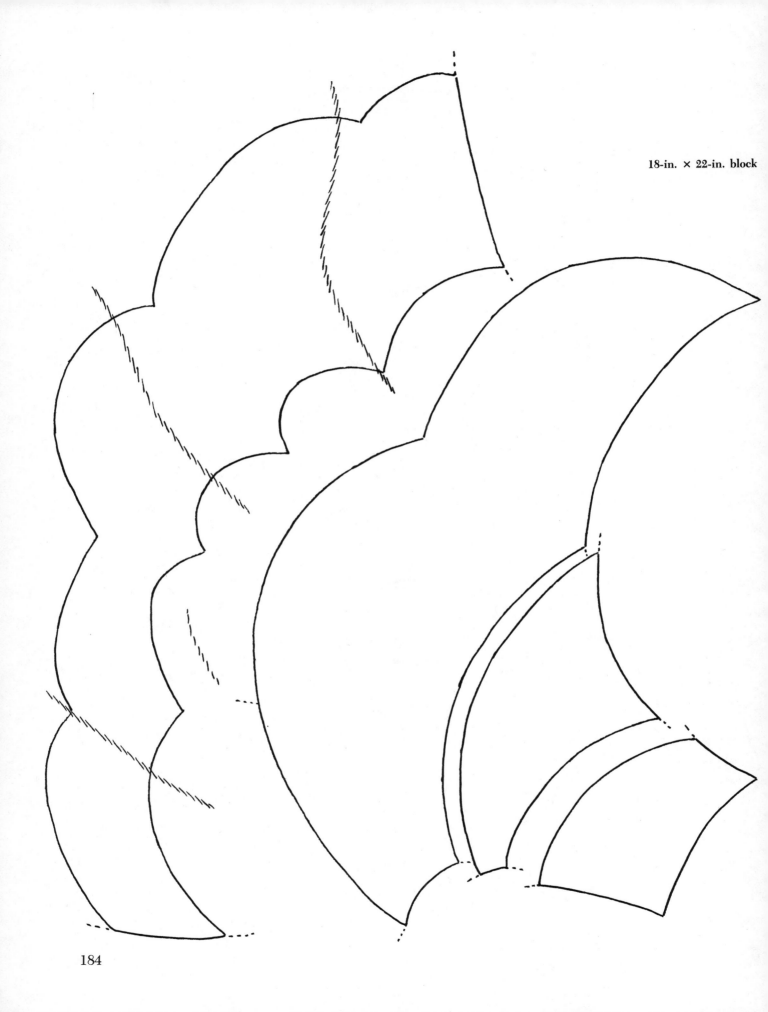

18-in. × 22-in. block

184

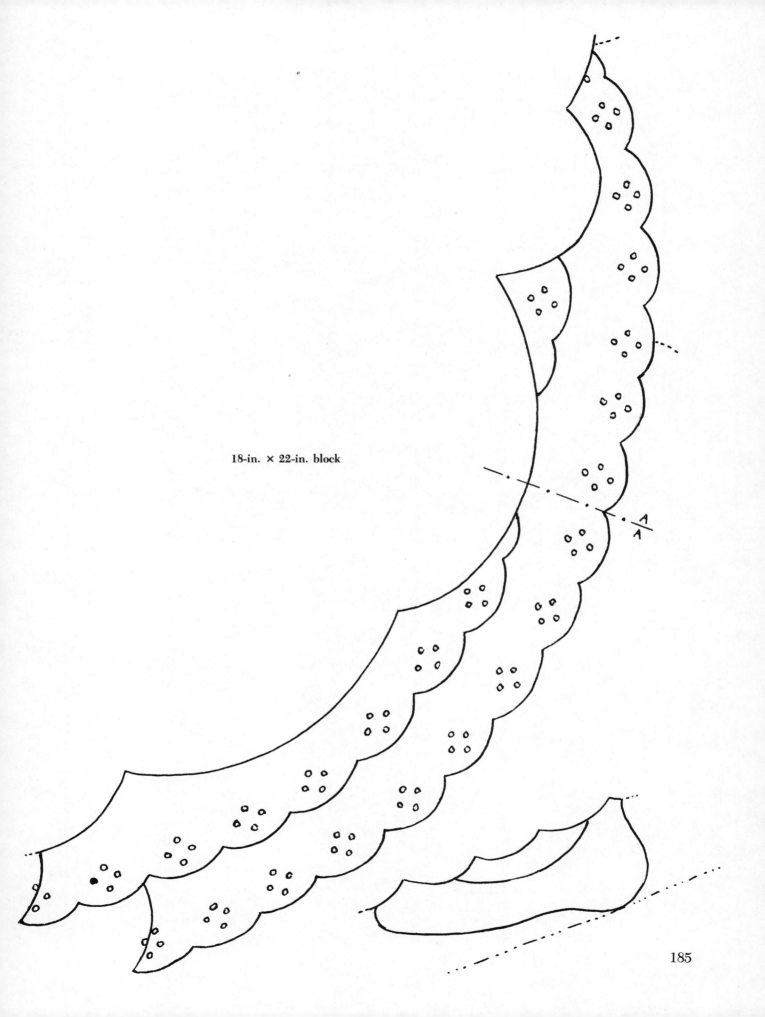

18-in. × 22-in. block

A
A

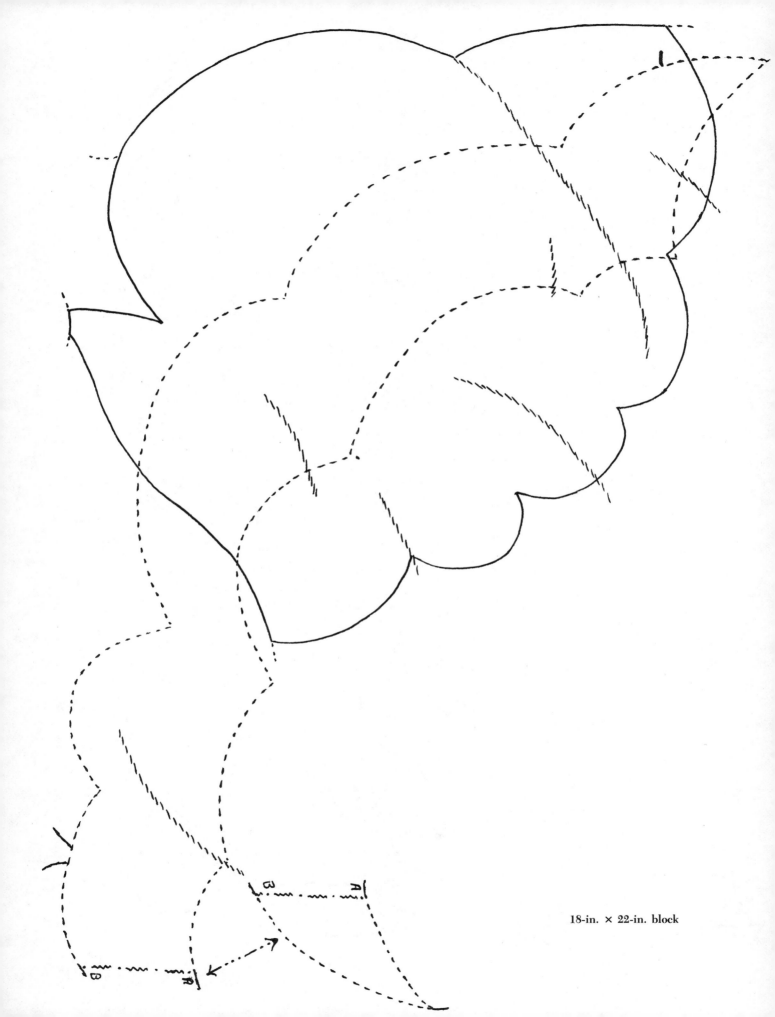

18-in. × 22-in. block

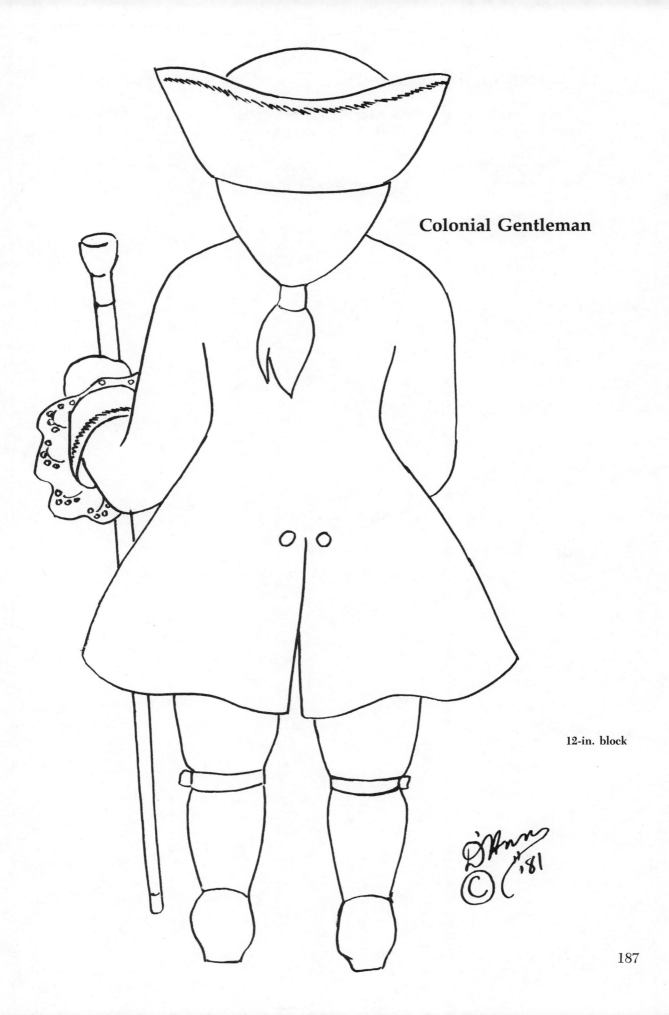

Colonial Gentleman

12-in. block

187

Colonial Gentleman—1981

When I finished arranging the Sunbonnet patterns for this manuscript, the first thing I noticed was that the Colonial patterns were all of girls and women. So, I decided to add this Gentleman to accompany them.

The patterns are drawn for 12-inch square blocks in embroidery or appliqué with embroidered trim, and for an 18"-by-22" oblong quilt center in appliqué with embroidery trim.

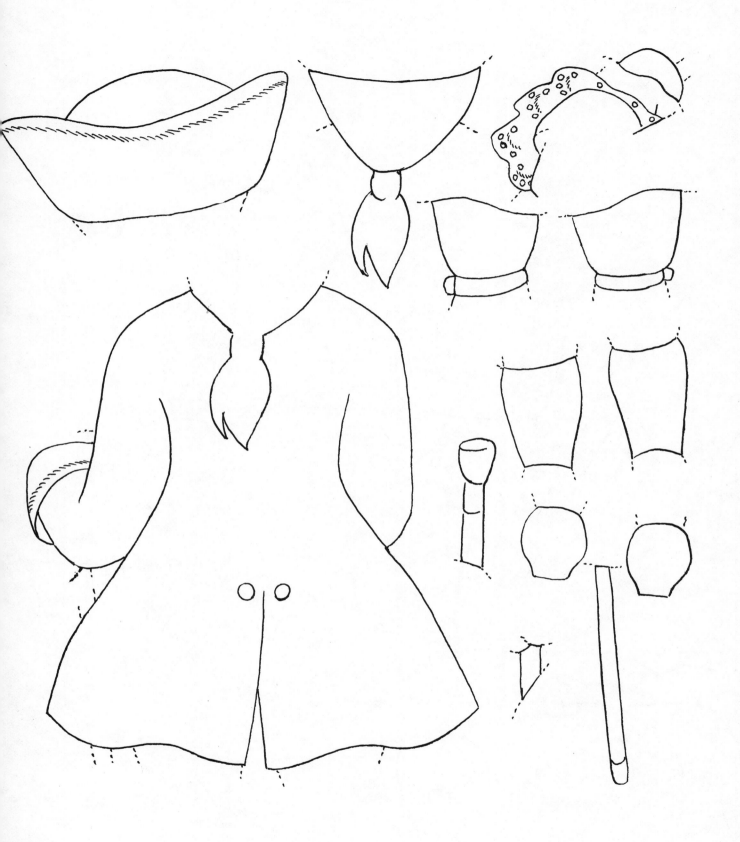

12-in. block

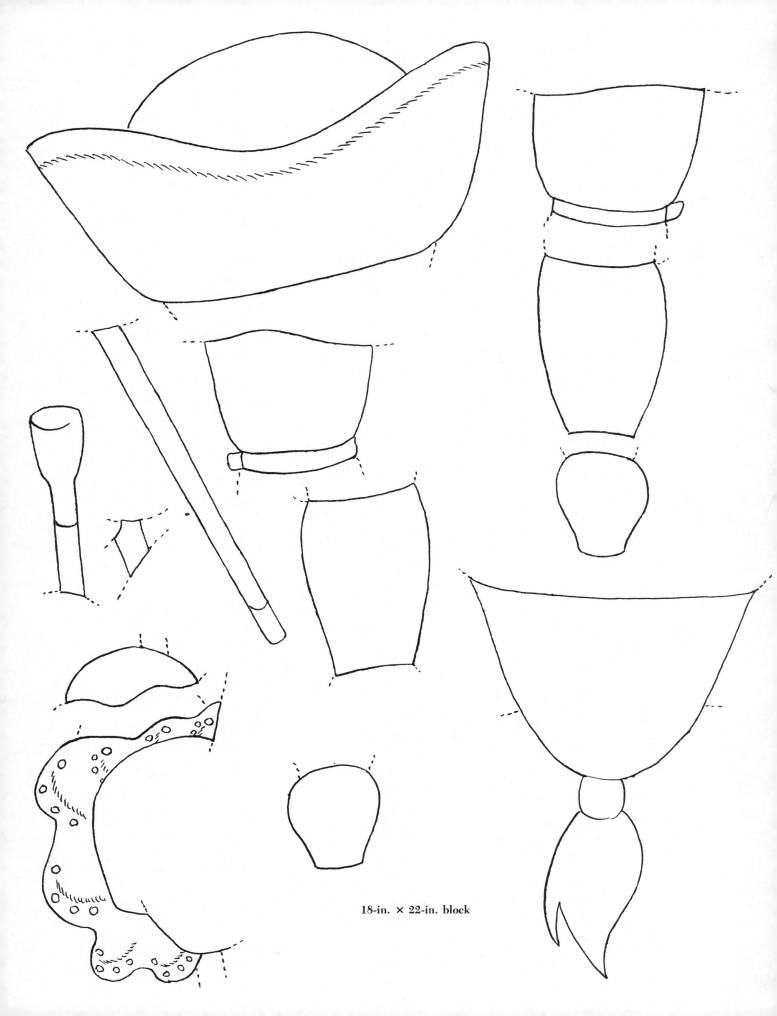

18-in. × 22-in. block

18-in. × 22-in. block

12-in. block

192

The Colonial Belle—1920

This is one of the most elaborate Colonial Lady designs I have found. This lady was designed for a pillow, but she would also be cute on a quilt block.

The patterns are drawn for a 12-inch square in either embroidery or for appliqué with embroidered trim, and for a 15-inch square in appliqué with embroidery trim.

12-in. block

194

15-in. block

195

15-in. block

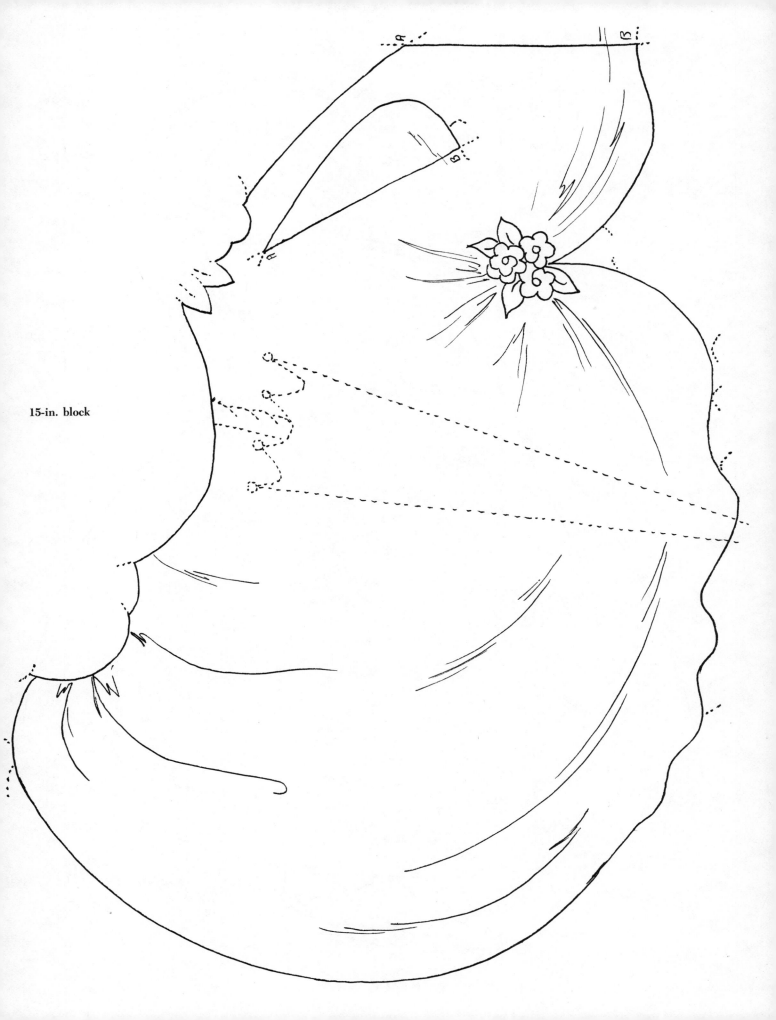

15-in. block

Dolley

12-in. block

198

Colonial Dolley and
Colonial Mollie—1921

This is another pair of pillow designs from *Woman's World* magazine that will make charming quilt pattern designs as well. The originals were appliquéd, and then the flowers and details were embroidered in large, simple stitches.

The patterns are drawn for 12-inch squares in either embroidery or appliqué with embroidery, and 18-inch squares for appliqué with embroidery. If the scarf, petticoat, and pantalette edges on Mollie seem too intricate for appliqué, you might prefer to substitute slightly ruffled lace edging. Placed diagonally, the figures fit on 10-inch and 15-inch blocks.

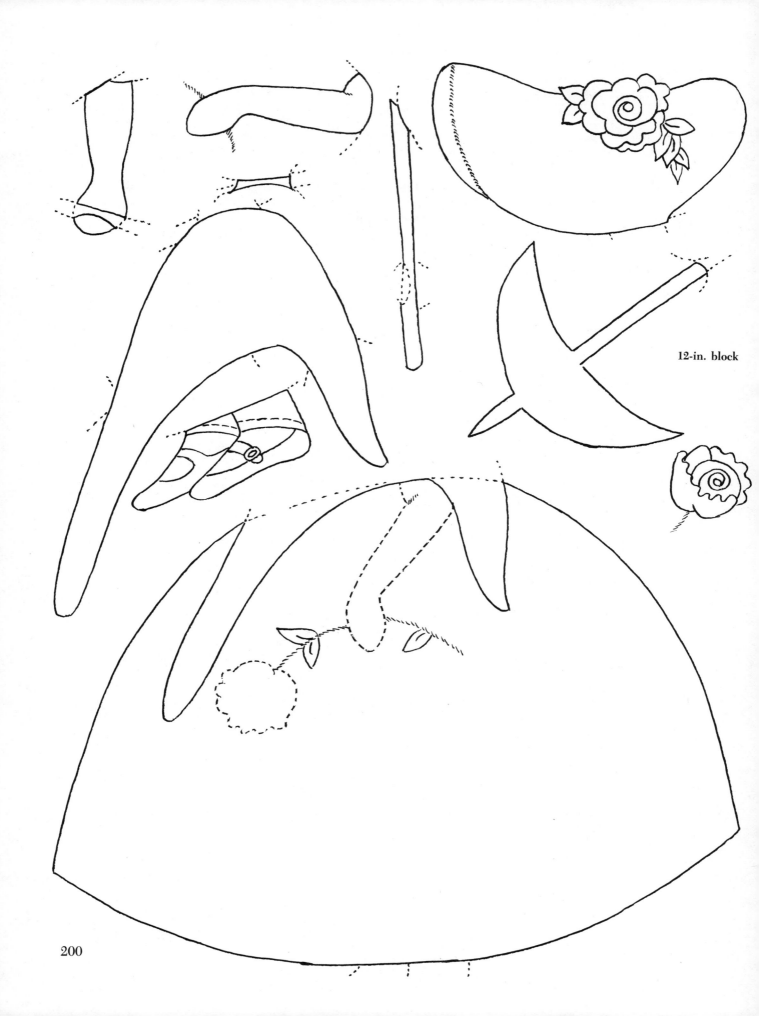

12-in. block

200

18-in. block

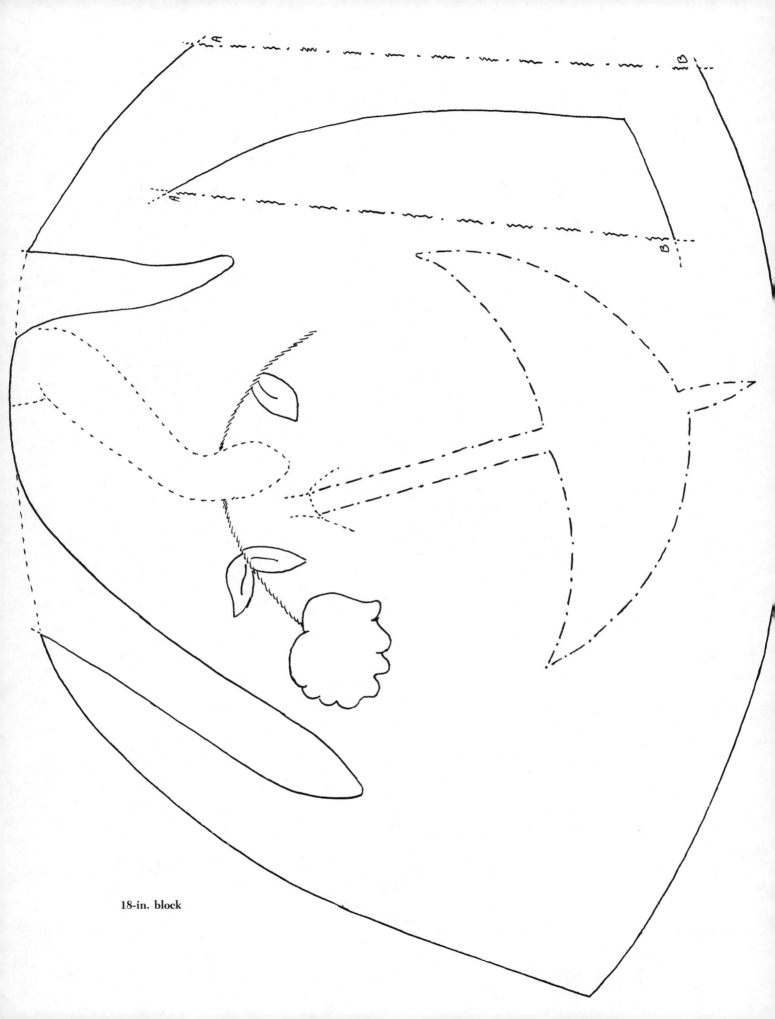

18-in. block

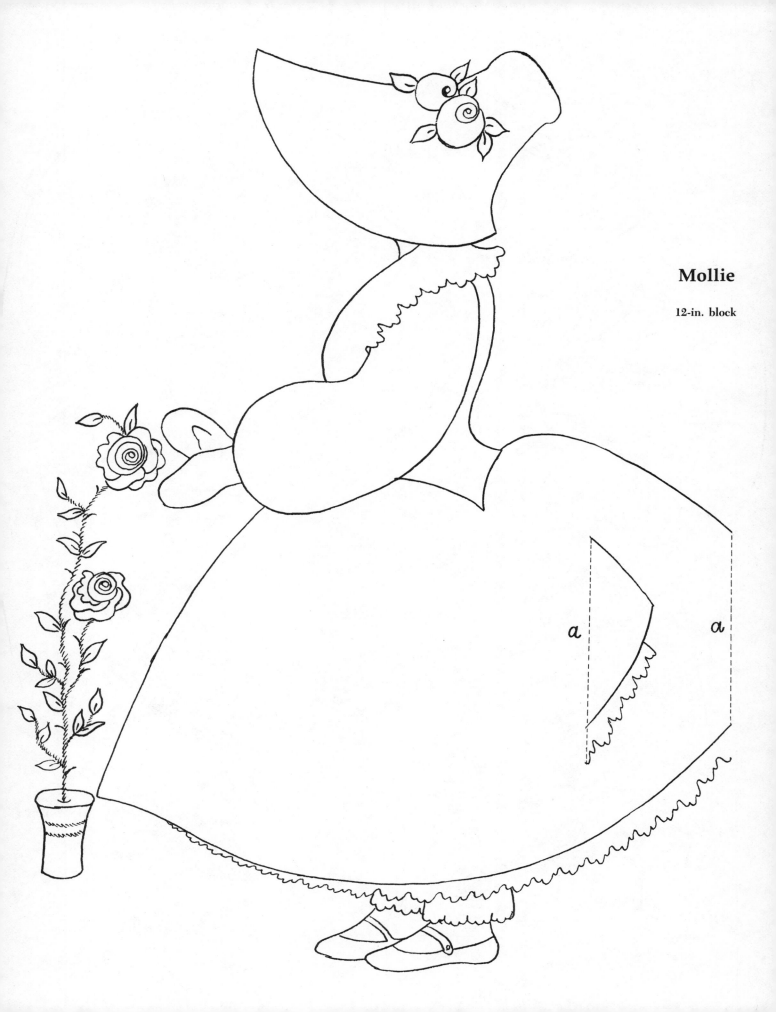

Mollie

12-in. block

a   *a*

12-in. block

204

18-in. block

18-in. block

Federal Lass

12-in. block

207

A Federal Lass—1921

This pattern and the next were published together in another *Woman's World* column. They are most unusual in having the Empire costumes of the 1820's rather than the usual wide-skirted styles of most of the other designs.

The patterns are drawn for 12-inch square blocks in embroidery or appliqué with embroidery, and for 15-inch square blocks in appliqué with embroidery trim. Remember to add three raindrops in the larger size even though the pattern gives only one.

12-in. block

15-in. block

210

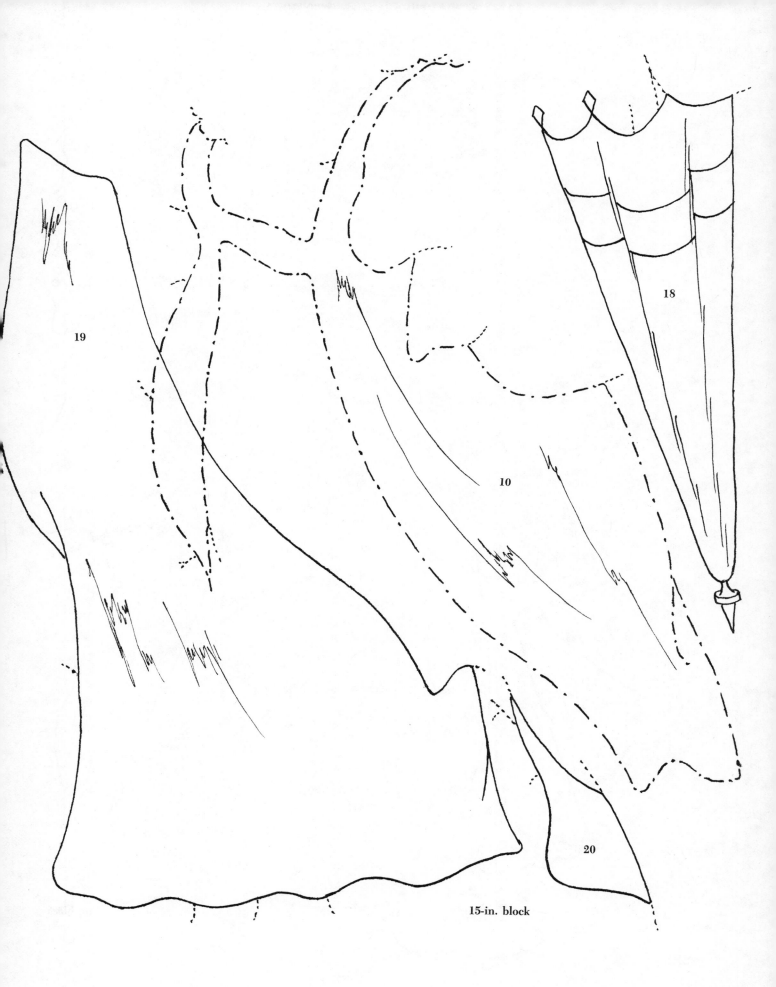

19

10

18

20

15-in. block

12-in. block

212

The Snow Child—1921

A companion pattern to the Federal Lass, this shows Winter in contrast to the previous pattern's Summer. I think the designer's mistake in giving this girl the anachronistic 1920's galoshes when the remainder of her clothing is in the style of the 1820's is adorable.

The patterns are drawn for 12-inch square blocks in either embroidery or appliqué with embroidered trim, and for 18-inch square blocks in appliqué with embroidered trim. The fancy snowflake designs should be copied for the background of the larger-sized design. You can add a flake or two if you wish. Placed diagonally, the figures fit on 10-inch and 15-inch blocks.

12-in. block

214

18-in. block

215

18-in. block

Country Maid

12-in. block

217

Country Maid and
City Lady—1975

A friend needed patterns for two Kate Greenaway-like designs for a pair of children's quilts. These patterns are the result.

The patterns are drawn for 12-inch square blocks in either embroidery or appliqué with embroidery trim, and 18"-by-22" oblong quilt centers in appliqué with embroidery trim.

A.

B.

C.

D.

E.

F.

G.

H.

I.

J.

12-in. block

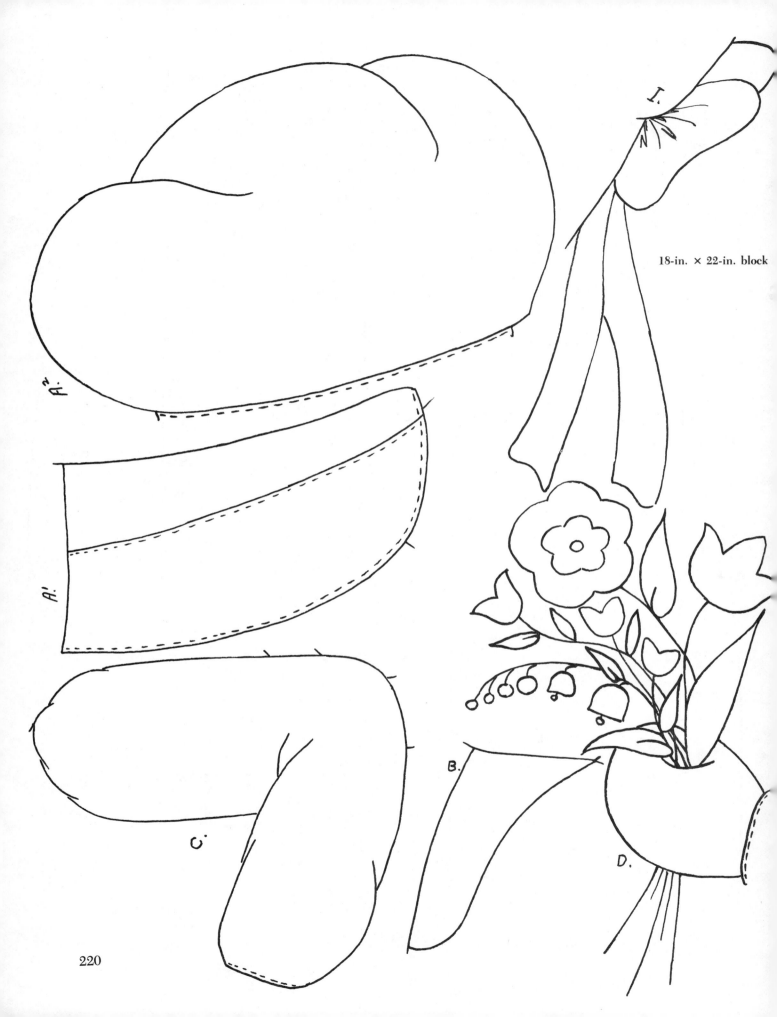

18-in. × 22-in. block

220

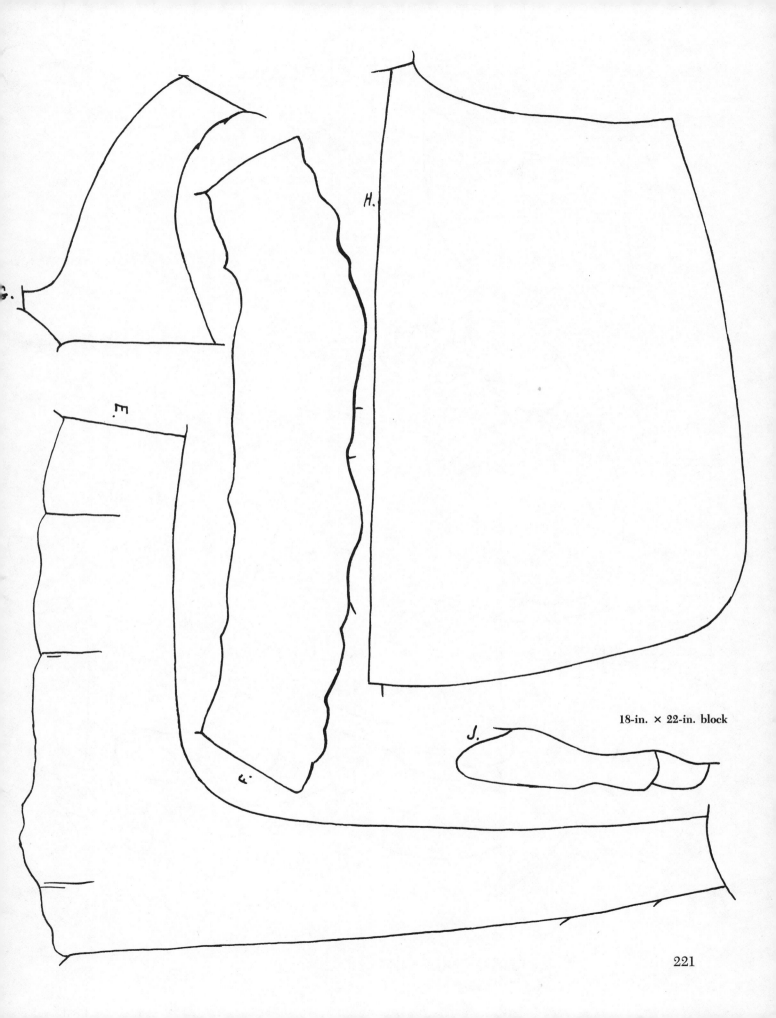

G.

E.

H.

F.

J.

18-in. × 22-in. block

221

City Lady

12-in. block

$A.^1$

$A.^2$

$A.^3$

B.

D.^{1}

D.^{2}

D.^{3}

J.

K.

18-in. × 22-in. block

224

18-in. × 22-in. block

225

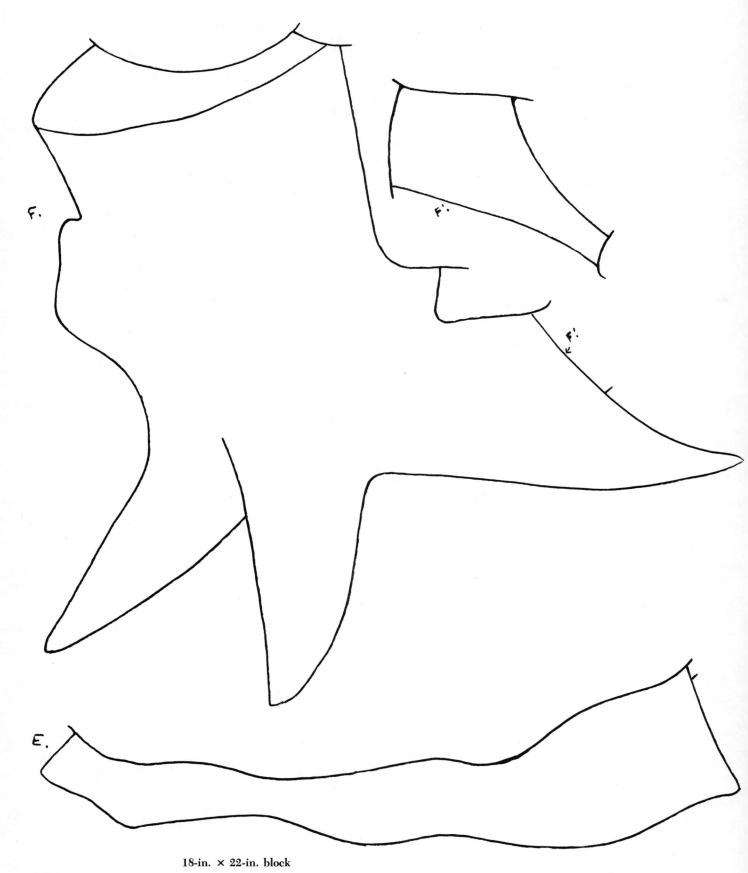

F.

F'.

F'.

E.

18-in. × 22-in. block

10-in. block

Maiden on a Swing

Maiden on a Swing—1940's

The only block design from the 1916 4-H series of quilt patterns (see also Sunbonnet Susy, page 138) that interested quilters enough to last was the "Sunbonnet on a Swing" design. There have been many subsequent versions created over the years, but this dainty Colonial bonnet lady is my favorite.

The patterns have been drawn for a 10-inch-square block size in embroidery or appliqué and embroidery trim, in 12-inch-square block size for appliqué with embroidery trim, and in 18-inch-square block size in appliqué with embroidery trim.

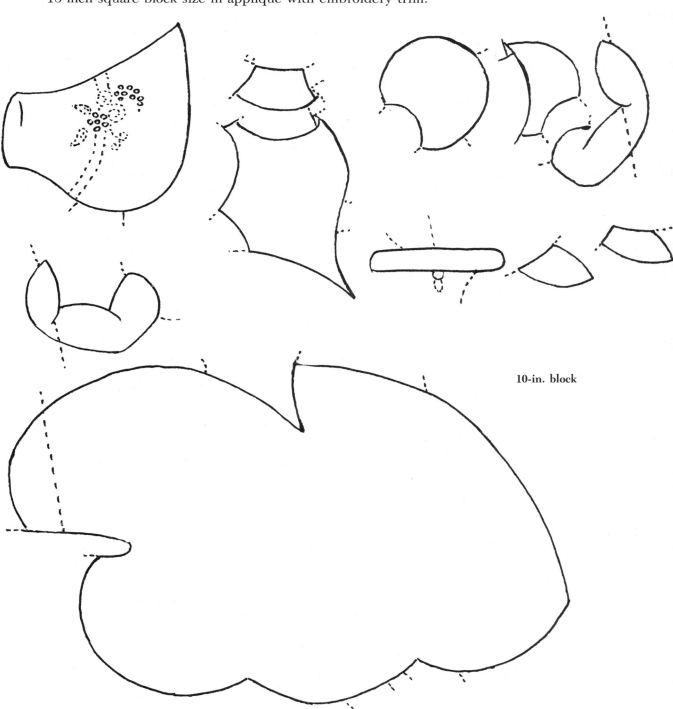

10-in. block

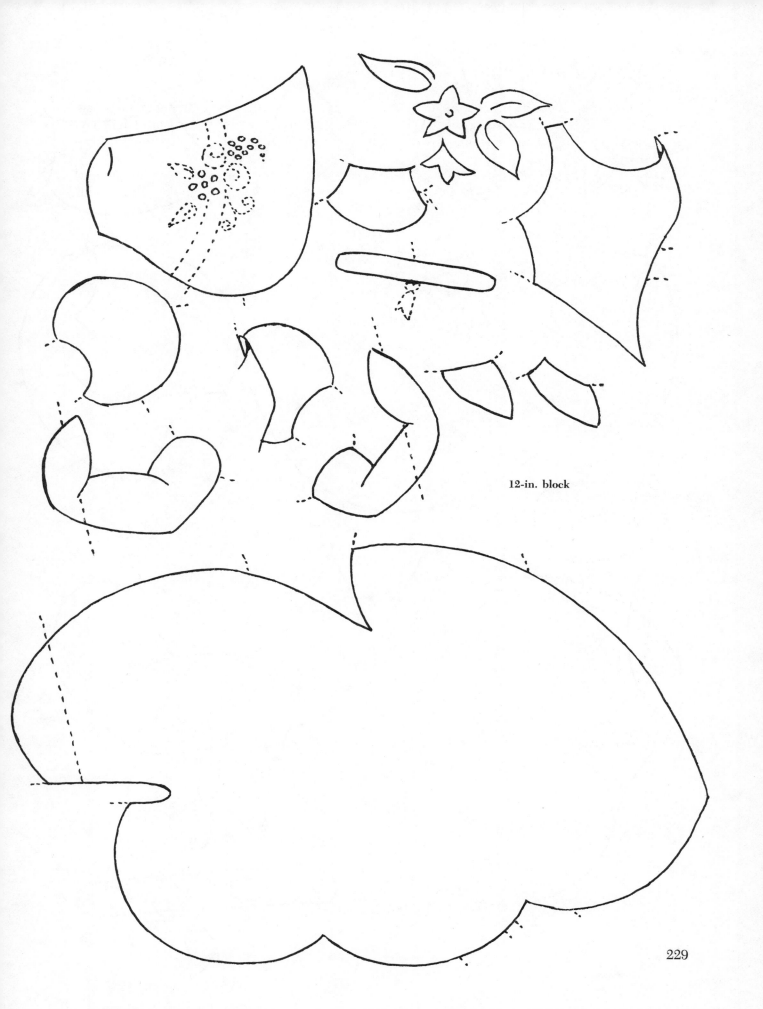

12-in. block

229

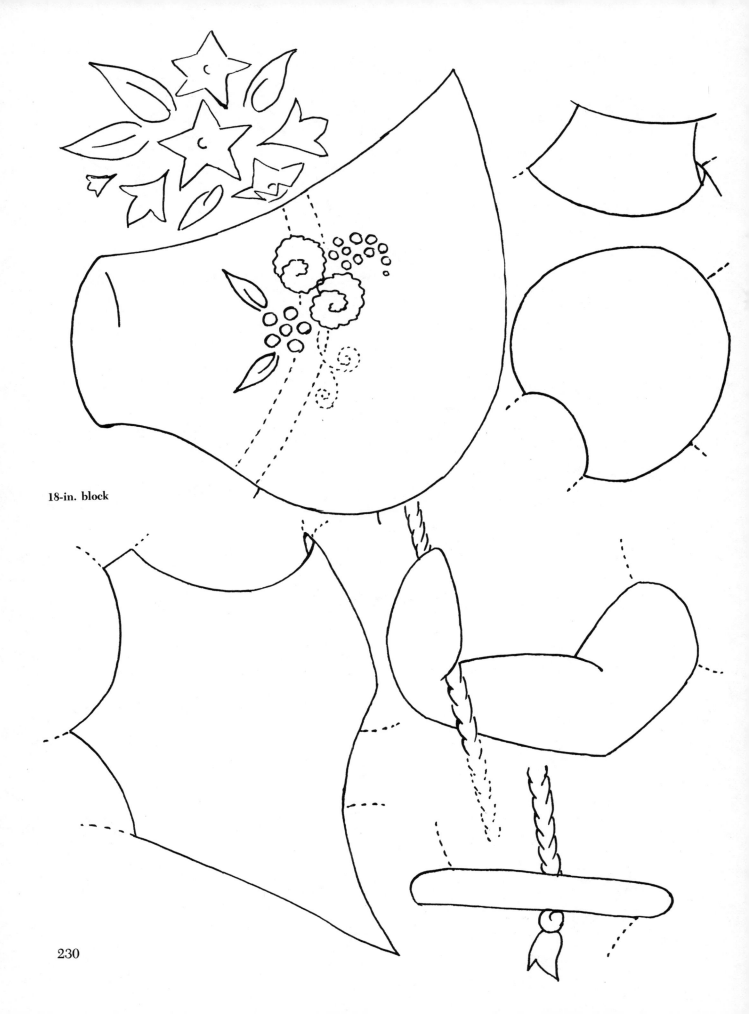

18-in. block

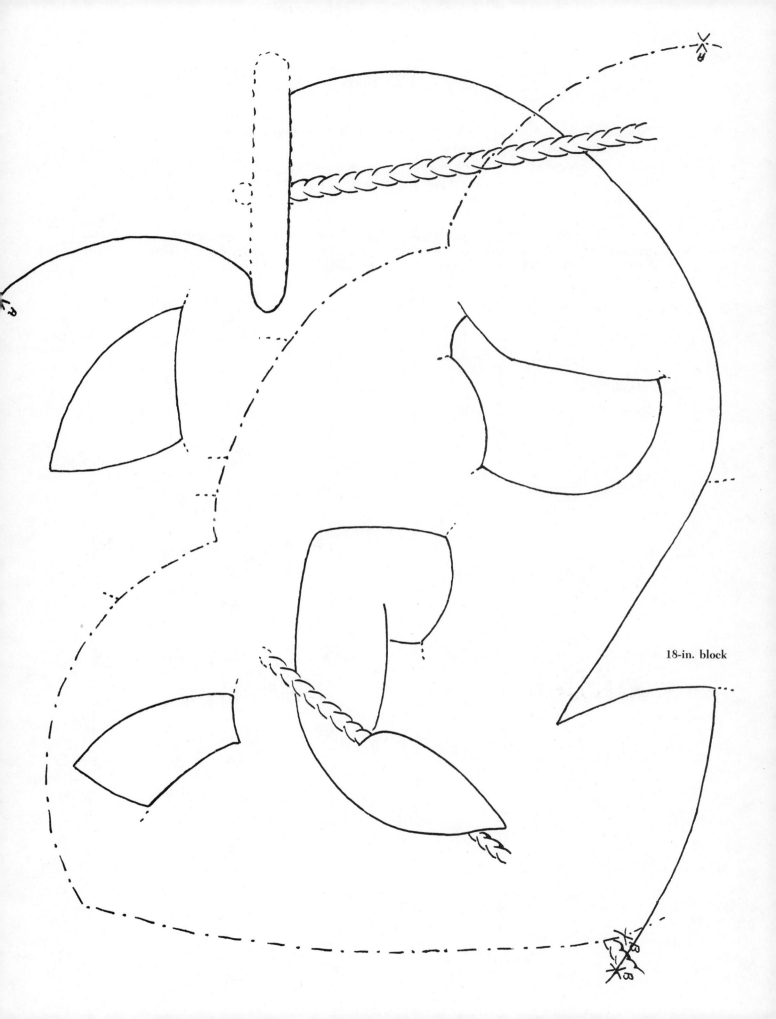

18-in. block

Colonial Lady—1920's

   This pattern has been popular since the 1920's, but this particular design was taken from a 1930 pattern book. You can make a quilt from the six designs, each represented eight times, or you can make a whole quilt from one or two of the designs. This quilt will look best with three-inch lattice strips between the blocks. It is a scrap quilt design. The dotted-line patterns are meant to be embroidered on the squares, while the solid-line patterns must be cut out and appliquéd. Each dress should have a print and a matching, solid-colored trim. Finished blocks should be 15 inches square when the appliqué is positioned as shown. If the appliqué is placed diagonally on the square, 12-inch squares can be used. A twin-bed quilt should be composed of six rows of eight blocks each.

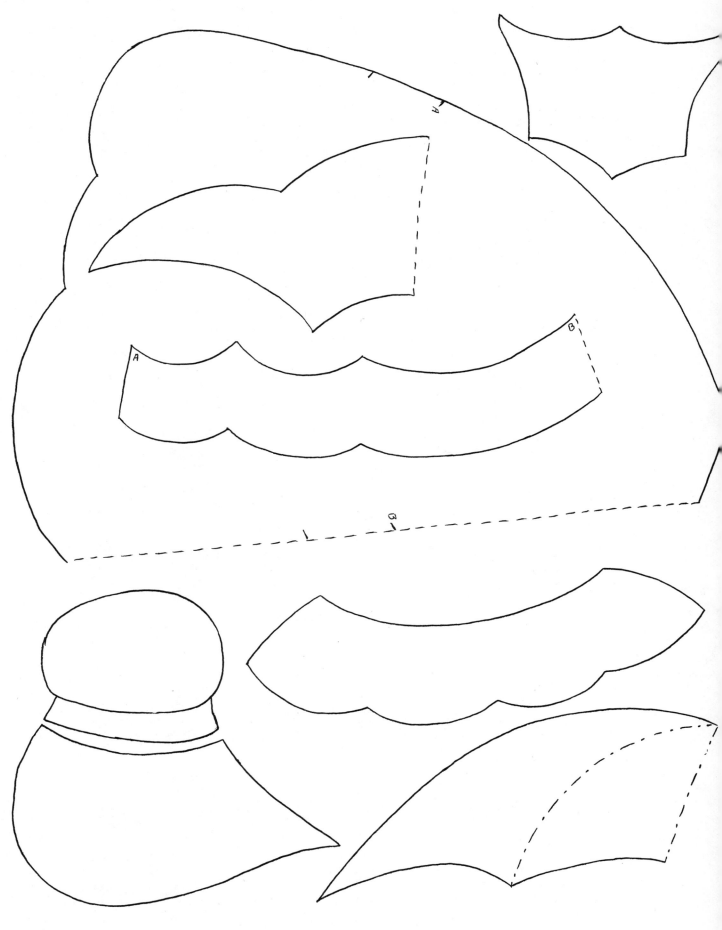

Mary Christmas—1911

The easiest place to find a variety of good examples of early Sunbonnet types is among old postcards. The last antique postcard I bought was a Christmas Greeting card with this charming little girl on the front. The design was signed "M. Dulk," and the postmark was 1911. The design was so appealing I knew I had to redraw it as a pattern.

There are two patterns for embroidery—one for an 8-inch and the other for a 12-inch square block. Also included are nineteen pattern pieces for appliqué on a 12-inch square block.

8-in. block

12-in. block

12-in. block

While there's Christmas in the air
Christmas greeting everywhere
I am sending this to you.
Merry Christmas.

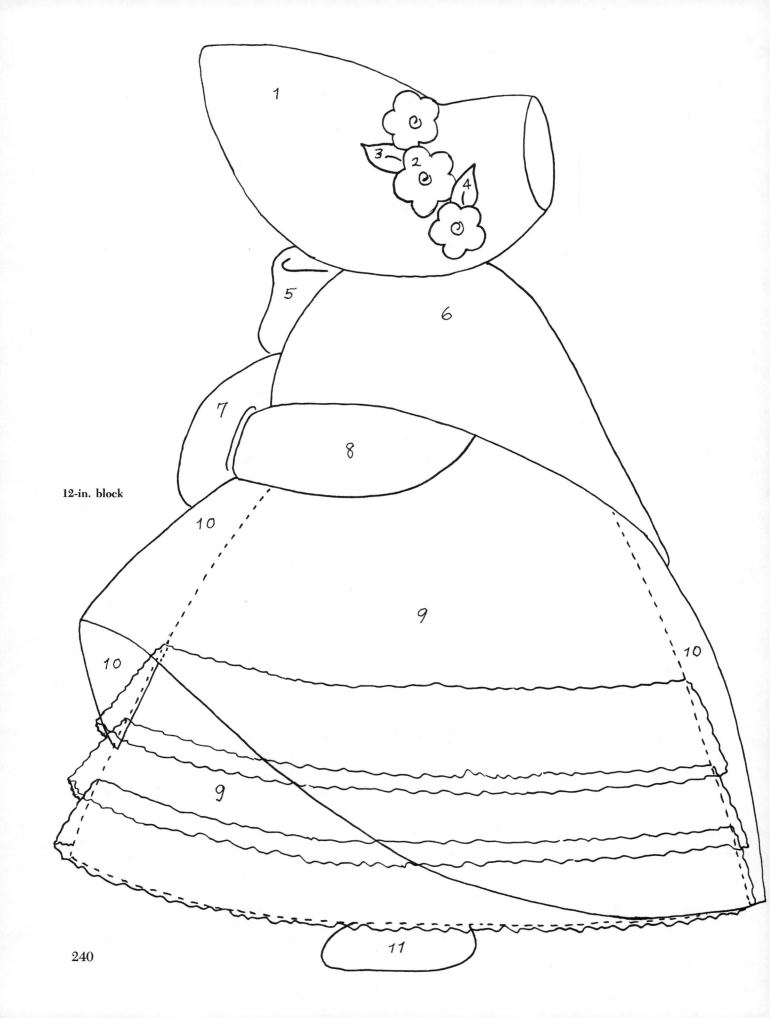

12-in. block

240

The Victorian Miss—1933

This is an interesting variation in Sunbonnet designs. Most patterns are one-dimensional designs, for use on flat pieces of material such as quilt blocks and pillow tops. But this pattern was designed to be used as a pajama bag, with the full overskirt hiding the bag opening. The pattern is complicated. Read it through *before* you begin to be sure you understand the procedure.

First, make the bag itself. Make a newspaper or brown-paper-bag pattern for piece 9 by enlarging the diagram given, following the shape and dimensions shown. Use the enlarged pattern to cut two of pattern 9 from fairly sturdy material. Make a 5½-inch slit in one of the two, as shown in the illustration on page 244. Finish the raw edges by rolling them under and whip-stitching to the wrong side of the fabric. Turn the triangular flaps at top and bottom under and fasten them securely. You may want to reinforce the slit opening by running seam binding around the edges—especially at the bottom corner. Join the two bag pieces together, sewing right sides together at sides and bottom, but leaving the bottom seam open between the large dots for the shoe. Clip corners and turn right sides out. Top-stitch the sides and bottom, except where you have left the seam open. Set aside.

To make the three-dimensional figure: Fold your pieces of material in half, right sides together. Cut out two pieces each (at the same time) of patterns 1, 5, 6, 7, 8, and 11 (one set will be reversed). Piece the two half-figure sets together; then place their right sides together and stitch around the edges, leaving the waist area (the lower edges of pieces 6 and 8) free. Clip curves and turn: then stuff lightly. Pin the bottom edges closed to keep the stuffing in place, turning the seam allowance under. Then set this aside also.

Enlarge the diagram for pattern 10 (the overskirt), again following the shape and dimensions shown. *Notice that pattern 10 includes seam allowances, unlike any of the other pattern pieces in this book* (c). Cut one skirt from this pattern. Join the two short edges of the rectangle, right sides together, to make a tube shape. Finish the skirt hem. The vertical lines on the top edge of the skirt indicate gathering (b). Gather the skirt loosely at the top until you can fit the gathered edge around the unfinished top edge of the bag comfortably. Sew the overskirt to the top edge of the bag, matching *a* dots for placement.

Remove the pins from the lower edge of the stuffed half-figure *just enough* to insert the lower half of the figure (skirt and bag) into the opening—being careful to keep the stuffing in place. Pin securely (again to hold the stuffing) and then sew the two halves of the figure together along the lower edges of pattern pieces 6 and 8. The stuffed upper half of the figure will then be completely sealed off. The slit in the pajama bag will be completely hidden under the overskirt.

Finish the lower half of the figure: Take the two fabric pieces cut from pattern 11 and sew them right sides together for the shoe, leaving the ankle seam free. Clip curves, turn, and stuff lightly; then insert the raw edges into the space left in the lower edge of the pajama bag and sew the shoe in place in such a way as to complete the top stitching around the pajama bag. Be sure that you point the toes in the right direction!

Last, finish the fine details, which really make this pattern special. Prepare two sets of flowers and leaves cut from patterns 2, 3, and 4 for appliqué, clipping curves and basting down raw edges. Appliqué these to the bonnet. You may want to add a flower or leaf to extend the bonnet trim over the crown of the bonnet, which is now slightly curved from having been stuffed. Finally, add ruffles to the pajama bag to make the actual bag portion a petticoat, at lines marked *d* on pattern 9.

These directions are for an 18-inch-high p.j. bag. The other pattern is drawn for a 12-inch-square block in embroidery. It can be divided easily for appliqué with embroidery.

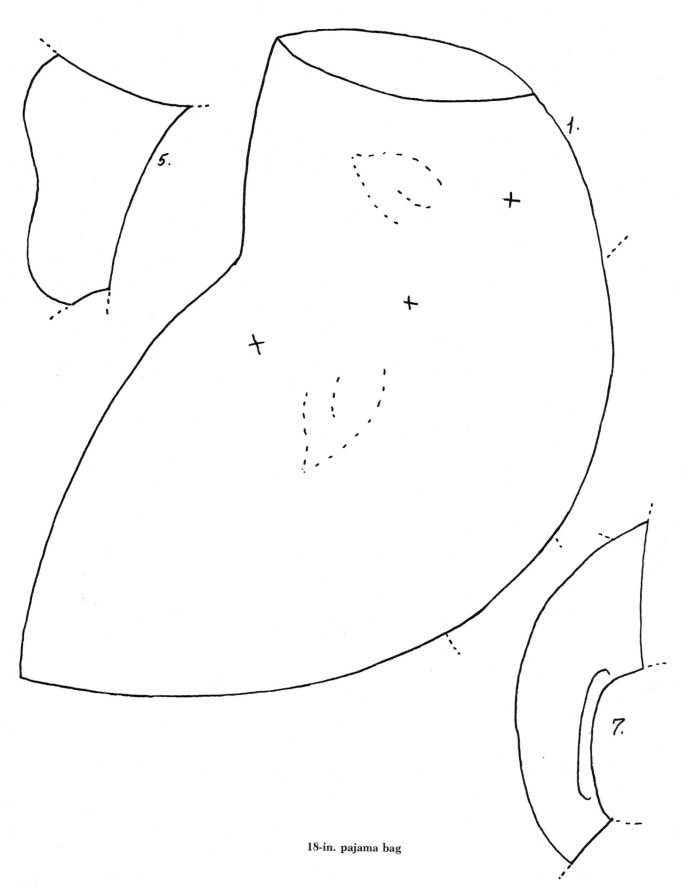

5.

1.

7.

18-in. pajama bag

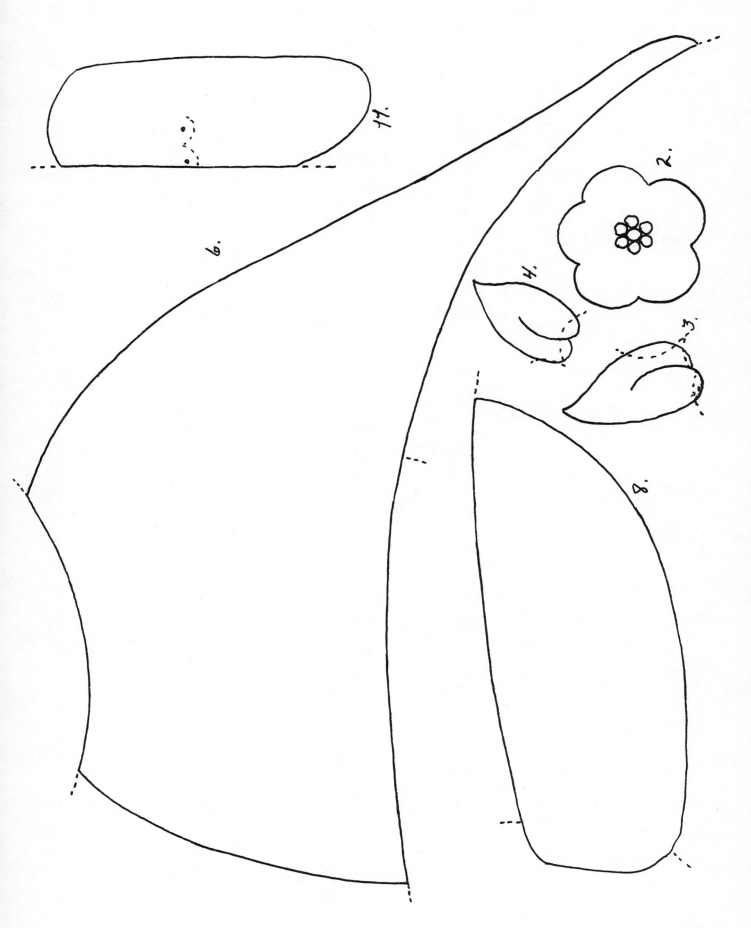

243

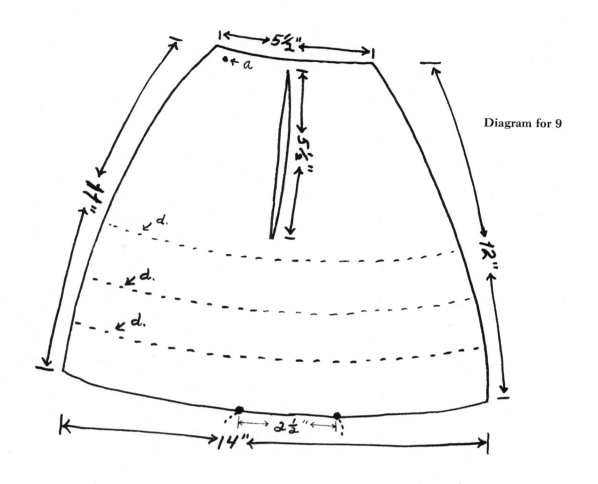

Diagram for 9

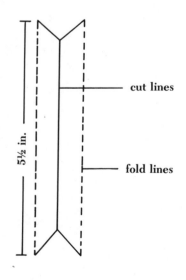

cut lines

fold lines

5½ in.

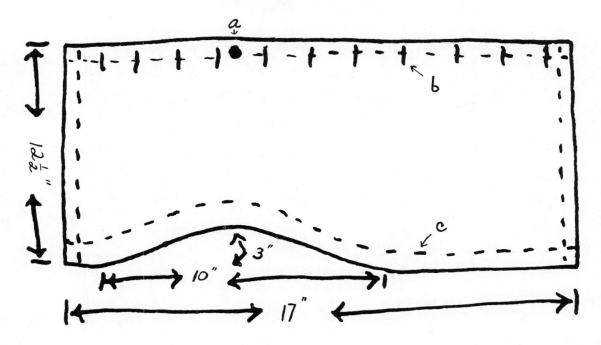

a: match skirt to *a* on piece 9

b: gathering marks

c: seam allowance

d: attach ruffles to petticoat

Greenaway Bonnet Girl—1880's

A slight turn of the head made this design perfect as a Sunbonnet type.

Most of the early Sunbonnets and Greenaway designs used on quilts were outline-embroidered. This pattern is drawn to be used in the original manner. It will fit on a 12-inch square block.

10-in. block

(a)

Sally in a Hurry—1940's

One of my Maryland friends gave this pattern to me—and she wasn't even a quilter. I have had it for about twenty years, and have not seen it in any other collection or book. Judging from the style, it must have been designed after World War II. The original was appliquéd on the diagonal of the block.

The patterns are drawn for 10-inch square blocks (design placed straight) and 12-inch blocks. I have drawn both embroidery and appliqué-with-embroidery patterns in both sizes.

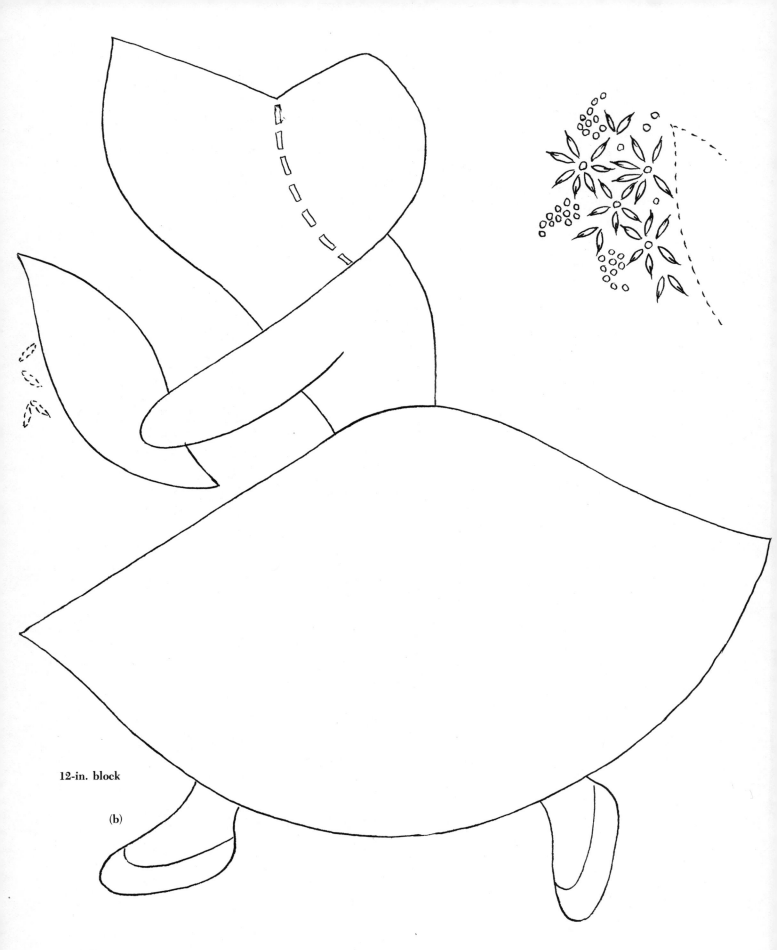

12-in. block

(b)

250

1a

1b

2a

a

3a

4b

5a

2b

5b

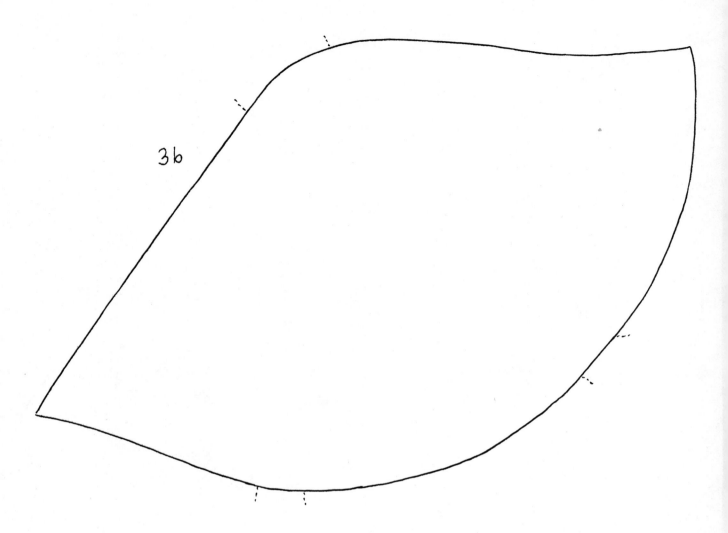

3b

252

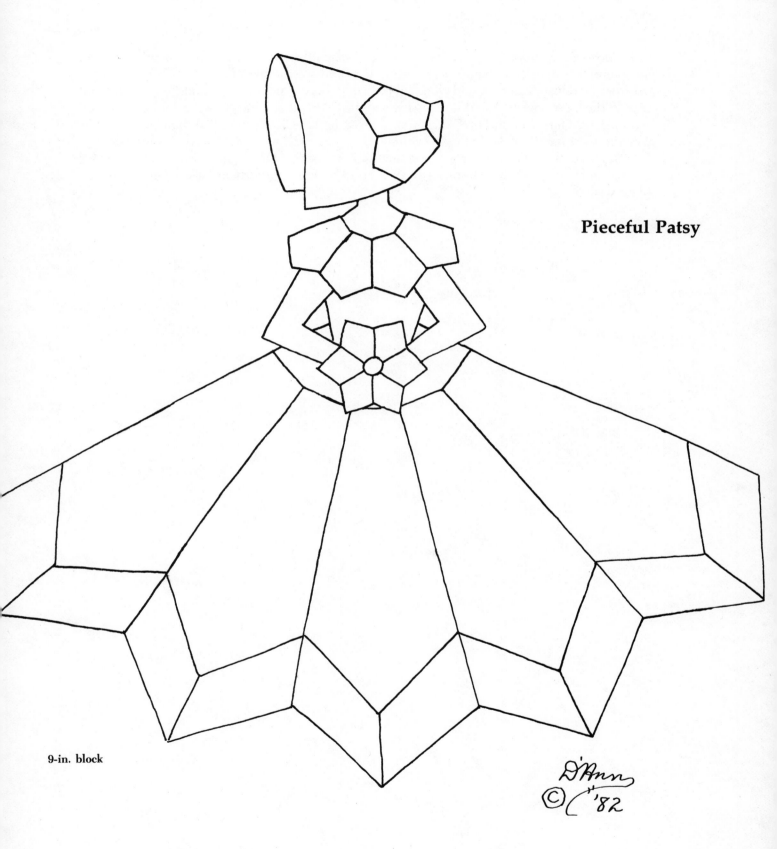

Pieceful Patsy

9-in. block

253

Pieceful Patsy—1982

This pieced Sunbonnet is one of the patterns I designed myself. There may be other pieced versions of this style, but I have never been able to find one for my collection. It is based on the Dresden Plate patch pattern and would make a cute border pattern for almost any quilt if the skirts of the figures were joined side by side and the remainder of the girl were appliquéd to the border strip. The lower part of the arms, the flower, and the flower center should be appliquéd over the skirt on all of the figures. The flower center can be embroidered if you wish.

The patterns are drawn for pieced 9-inch square blocks. Divide the pattern into units for this size and for pieced 12-inch square blocks. The 9-inch size pattern may also be embroidered if you wish.

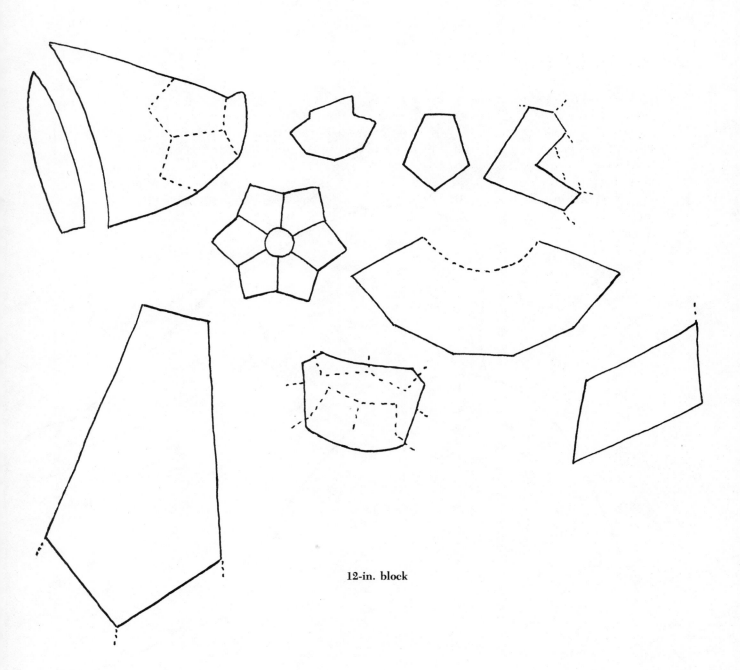

12-in. block

256

Nancy Runabout—1930's

Quilt patterns always reflect all shades of social opinion, because quilters agree on very little except their enjoyment of the art and craft of quilting. This vigorous figure has been in my collection for many years. I can't think of her as a Colonial; she is more of a Frontierswoman. Of course, she has become contemporary again, the very picture of a militant feminist. I have therefore added a pattern for a feminist poster that can be substituted for the original umbrella.

The patterns are drawn for 12-inch square blocks in either embroidery or appliqué with embroidery trim.

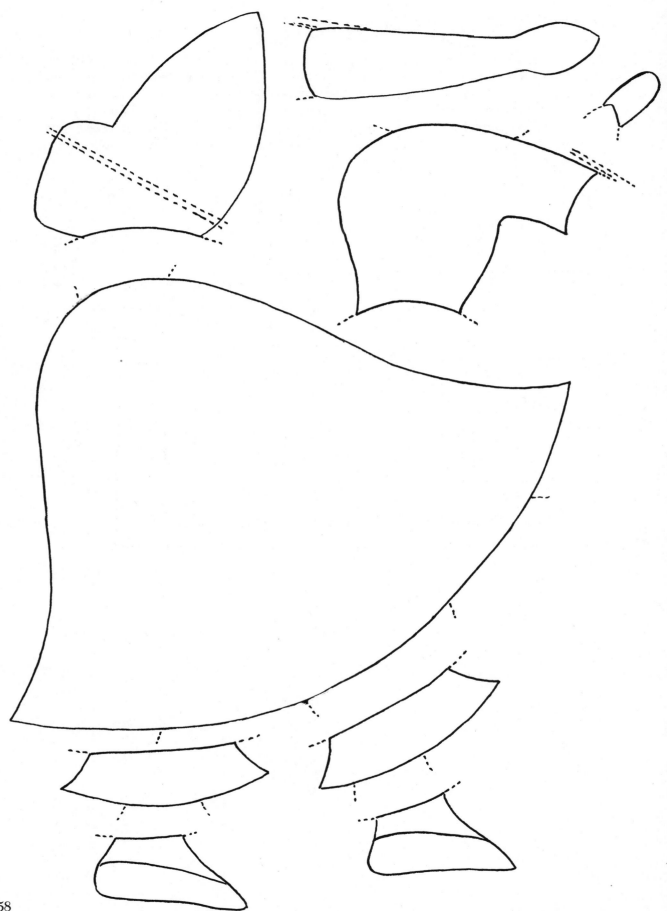

258

Acknowledgments

Many people have taken an interest in this book and have made a special contribution to it. I would like to express my appreciation to them here.

Several friends donated patterns, including Mrs. Cuesta Benberry of St. Louis, Missouri, and Mrs. Jeanne Hindman. Mrs. Beverly A. Orbelo of San Antonio, Texas, not only contributed to the patterns but also provided several items of her own to be photographed. Some of her work appears on the back jacket of this book. Mrs. Anita Murphy of Kountze, Texas, also brought me quilts and with Mrs. Orbelo helped to organize our photography sessions. Mrs. Murphy's remarkable "Life and Times" wall hanging (see color insert), as its name implies, is designed as an emblem of her own life. (Each of the small quilts on the clothesline denotes one of her grandchildren; the Sunbonnet quilt is 3½-inches by 3½-inches, and each Sunbonnet is one inch tall.) I am very grateful to all these women for the generous gift of their time and talents.

I would also like to express my appreciation to the Golden Triangle Quilting Guild of Beaumont, Texas, and to the Star Quilters of San Antonio, Texas; to Diane Herbort, Joanne Canestra, Mrs. Patricia Bergh, and Mrs. Mary Lou Gottschall, without whose efforts the photographic insert simply would not be.

Jim Nash of Austin, Texas, took the photographs for the book except those credited individually. His assistance—with this book and with others—has been invaluable.

260

Index of Patterns and Sizes

The traditional name for all but a few of these patterns is simply Sunbonnet Sue or Overall Bill. Since it would therefore be quite confusing for everyone if the patterns were all called by their traditional names, I have given each pattern its own, arbitrarily chosen, individual name.

NOTE: An asterisk (*) indicates original designs by the author that have never before been published.